ULSTER BLOOD

Michael Sheane

D0513109

ARTHUR H. STOCKWELL LTD.
Torrs Park   Ilfracombe   Devon
Established 1898
www.ahstockwell.co.uk

British Library Cataloguing-in-Publication Data.
A catalogue record for this book is available
from the British Library.

Arthur H. Stockwell Ltd. bears no responsibility
for the accuracy of events recorded in this book.

By the same author:
Ulster & Its Future After the Troubles (1977)
Ulster & The German Solution (1978)
Ulster & The British Connection (1979)
Ulster & The Lords of the North (1980)
Ulster & The Middle Ages (1982)
Ulster & Saint Patrick (1984)
The Twilight Pagans (1990)
Enemy of England (1991)
The Great Siege (2002)
Ulster in the Age of Saint Comgall of Bangor (2004)

ISBN 0 7223 3701-9
Printed in Great Britain by
Arthur H. Stockwell Ltd.
Torrs Park   Ilfracombe
Devon

Contents

Chapter 1

The Scene Is Set

James VI of Scotland became James I of England, Scotland and Ireland in 1603, but there was already a presence of Lowland Scots in Ulster. James Hamilton appears as an important figure, along with a fellow Scot, James Fullerton, who arrived in Ireland about 1587. We know little of Fullerton's origins, but he probably came from Ayrshire. We know little more about Hamilton: he was the son of a minister of Ayrshire, and he had a good education which included a university degree. He taught at a school in Glasgow but was dissatisfied with this, and he went abroad to make his fortune. His ship was blown into Dublin and there he remained for the next thirteen years, but he did not plan an Irish career. He established a school in the city and employed James Fullerton as an assistant.

Elizabeth I founded Trinity College, Dublin, in 1591. Hamilton was able to support Trinity College in its efforts to remain solvent, and he went on a mission for the college to collect money in such diverse places as Tuam in Ireland and York in England. The two schoolmasters, Hamilton and Fullerton, did not sever their relations with Scotland. They kept themselves informed of Scottish affairs, and acted as agents for James VI. Hamilton was very clever. James appointed him resident agent at the English court in 1600. There were two other Lowland Scots who lived in the English Pale in the closing years of Elizabeth I's reign. Robert Maxwell, later to be given the deanery of Armagh by James I seems to have acted as an agent for Scotland. Denis Campbell became Dean of Limerick in 1587. The inroads of Scotland into the English Pale were quite small. In the north of Ireland, English authority was weak but there were settlements of Islander Scots and Highlanders by the time Elizabeth died.

The history of Scots migration from the Isles and Highlands reached far back to the 13th century when the gallowglass mercenaries crossed the North Channel to support the Irish chiefs in their efforts to enforce the status quo. These mercenaries arrived in force, and in return for their services they were granted lands by the chiefs. The Scots mercenaries were integrated and absorbed into Irish society. In the second half of the 13th century the Scots again arrived — the "New Scots" to distinguish themselves from the earlier arrivals. Their visits were of small duration, and only occasionally did they settle in Ireland. Few remained in Ulster. There was a considerable Scottish penetration on the east coast of Ulster. During the 12th century a number of Norman families had settled in counties Antrim and Down. In the 14th century Margery Bisset married John Mor MacDonald, Lord of the Isles, and was heiress to two thirds of the Glynns of Antrim. Thus the Scots had a foothold in Ulster and could claim rights by English law. The Scots of the Glynns tried to establish their independence of the Lordship of the Isles rather than in settling their Irish estates. The Scottish king asserted his authority over the Lordship in the 1490s, and Scotland's interest grew. By the middle of the 16th century, not only had the Scots asserted their authority over parts of Antrim, but had begun to expand south. The Archbishop of Armagh wrote in 1558 that County Down was as English as any part of the Pale and was now under Irishmen and Scots.

By the middle of the 16th century the English government in Ireland had clashed little with the Scots, and English officials only entered Ulster occasionally. The Scots had not penetrated into those parts of Ireland controlled by the English. However, the Tudors started to tighten their grip upon the country, and this was ground for conflict. The Tudors expanded into Ireland by two methods. First, the Irish could surrender their lands under the system of "Surrender and Re-grant", but they should have respect for English law. Having now English titles the earls paid lip service to English law. Secondly, there was the method of outright conquest by the English. Neither method could be applied to eastern Ulster and the Scots who did not recognise English authority remained entrenched upon the land. There were movements to oust the unpopular Scots. In 1556 Lord Fitzwalter, later made earl of Sussex, arrived in the country as deputy, and he took decisive action. The English enacted laws to prevent the Scots becoming established in the north. In the parliament that met in 1556, an act was passed forbidding all contact with the Scots and making it treason to intermarry with them. Fitzwalter also proposed an expedition against the Scots and made plans to settle in Ulster.

Fitzwalter launched his expedition two years later, attacking the Isles and their settlements in County Antrim, but once the English left the area there was nothing to prevent the Scots from reoccupying the Isles. The only way to stop this was by establishing a colony in eastern Ulster. The Archbishop of Armagh suggested that the Irish should be turned against the Scots. He asserted that the Scots should never be allowed to have a foothold in Ireland. During Elizabeth's reign efforts had been made to dislodge the Scots, either by direct action or by efforts organised by the Archbishop of Armagh. The plantation, or colonisation, in the west of

Ulster might put an end to Scots efforts along the Antrim and Down littoral. In 1560 Queen Elizabeth agreed to make Sorley Boy MacDonnell, one of the MacDonnell chiefs, her subject. She did not carry this out until thirteen years later. In 1561 she granted Sorley Boy MacDonnell's elder brother, James MacDonnell of Dunyveg, a chief of the clan, all the lands between the River Bush and the Bann in North Antrim, commonly known as the Route. This was a situation that should obtain for twenty-one years: Sorley Boy should rule the territory and pay the rent. Thus Elizabeth had recognised MacDonnell's control over a part of Antrim outside of the Bisset presence in the Glens of Antrim. The reason for the toleration of the Scots in Antrim was that Shane O'Neill of Tyrone was hostile to the English. When O'Neill submitted in 1563 the English tolerance of the Scots in Antrim came to an end. She had proposed an attack upon the Scots which England welcomed. After a sudden attack the Scots were defeated; James MacDonnell and Sorley Boy being captured, the former dying from his wounds in captivity. O'Neill now tried to raid the English Pale but, desperate for support, he started to negotiate with the Scots, but the MacDonnells did not forget the death of their chief — they had murdered him and released Sorley Boy whilst negotiations were in progress.

Shane died in 1567, but there was little progress in the north. The main enemies were the O'Neills, the O'Donnells, the McQuillans (who held the Route before the Scots had penetrated it) and of course the MacDonnells of the Glens. The MacDonnells failed to separate into two groups — Angus MacDonnell of Dunyveg was the successor of his father, James MacDonnell of Dunyveg, and he became chief of the Clan Donnell South which controlled Islay and Kintyre. Angus still held the right to the Glens, but the leadership of the MacDonnells fell increasingly to Sorley Boy, whose main ambition was to assert ownership over the Route of North Antrim.

Angus's clan became more and more preoccupied with Scottish affairs, and he was unable to devote enough time to Irish affairs. The Scottish crown was asserting itself and a bitter feud developed between the McLeans of Duart and the MacDonnells over the land in Islay. The MacDonnells now fell prey to the Clan Campbell, led by Archibald, seventh Earl of Argyll. Both the McLeans and the Campbells were heirs to land in Ireland: Catherine McLean lived with Shane O'Neill between 1561 and 1567, during which time they had two sons. By 1589 these sons, with the help of their clan in Scotland, were able to try to establish leadership over the O'Neills of Tyrone. Another woman, named Agnes, daughter of the fourth Earl of Argyll became involved with the Campbells. Agnes married James MacDonnell of Dunyveg and was the mother of Angus of Dunyveg, but her connection with Ireland did not end with James MacDonnell. In 1569 she married Shane O'Neill's successor, Turlough Luineach, and she brought with her about a thousand mercenaries as a dowry. At about the same time her daughter married the O'Donnell chief. For the next twenty years Agnes was found to be advancing the interest of her husband as well as her son by James MacDonnell. The marriage alliance alarmed England, and various schemes were set afoot, including the release of Mary Queen of Scots in return for a castle in Galloway. Colonisation was put forward as a major possibility. The Crown forfeited many lands, and this culminated in an attempt to settle Ulster in the early 1570s.

The first colonisation attempt was made in 1571: Sir Thomas Smith and his son received grants of territory in the Ards and Scots of Clandeboye in North Down, but only after a year the colony expired. Sir Thomas met his death at the hands of Irishmen in his own employ. It seemed for a moment that Queen Elizabeth accepted the position of the Scots: Sorley Boy MacDonnell accepted tenantries from the Crown and recognised the English position in Ulster. Walter Devereux, Earl of Essex, proposed to settle upon MacDonnell lands, and Elizabeth gave the scheme her blessing. However, this project made no more progress than the previous colonisation attempts. Now the MacDonnells remained in practical if not legal possession of Antrim. The Lord Deputy of Ireland urged an unsuccessful campaign against the MacDonnells in 1586. In May 1586 Angus MacDonnell was confirmed in possession of the Glens of Antrim. The McQuillans remained in possession of a part of North Antrim. Sorley Boy was granted the most fertile part of the Route.

Sorley Boy died in 1590. He was succeeded by his son, James, under whom the MacDonnells continued to expand their lands. In 1593 they seized part of the Route which was in the hands of the McQuillans, whose ancestry could be traced back to the Middle Ages. Now the Earl of Tyrone, Hugh O'Neill, tried to oust the English from Down and Antrim, a position that was obtained in 1594. Tyrone looked to the Scots of the Isles for help, where he found a friend in Angus MacDonnell of Dunyveg. The McLeans, who feuded with the MacDonnells, hated Tyrone since he had murdered one of the sons of Catherine McLean in 1689. They had made a bid for leadership over the O'Neills. The Scots of Islay sent help to Tyrone, probably in 1595, for they feared the McLeans.

Angus MacDonnell helped Tyrone because he expected some return against the McLeans. The Antrim MacDonnells did not involve themselves in disputes in the Isles, and they also avoided commitments to those English who came to Ulster. James MacDonnell protested loyalty to Elizabeth, and appealed for the release of his brother, Randal, who was being held as a pledge in Dublin. Tension now heightened between Tyrone and James MacDonnell, for as earl he had supported the McQuillans' efforts to regain their lost territory. Randal left Dublin and, in June, MacDonnell made a truce with Tyrone. Now Tyrone left the MacDonnells to their own devices, so that their control over the Route was absolute.

Also, in the same year, James VI of Scotland launched an attack against Angus of Dunyveg. The Antrim MacDonnells sized the Glens of Antrim from some of their clansmen. Angus wanted to resist the Scottish Crown and the Antrim chiefs supported him. But Angus was forced to submit in November 1596 without any force from England used against him. James MacDonnell had claims to Scottish territory, which James resisted. By 1596 James MacDonnell had control over the Route and the Glens. He posed some threat to the English, and he was a Roman Catholic so he might send Spaniards into Ireland. James MacDonnell eventually died in 1561, probably as the result of poison.

Randal succeeded his brother as chief of the Antrim MacDonnells, and he had little difficulty in retaining the territory taken from his brother. Tyrone remained powerful in the north, and Randal cooperated with him at Kinsale in 1601. He eventually submitted to the lord deputy when the English had ejected the Spaniards, and when Tyrone's cause was lost. In fact Randal had more to fear from his relatives in the Isles than from the English or the Irish. The MacDonnell presence in Scotland now seemed to be lost. Randal MacDonnell was in a strong position when James VI became King of England. He obtained huge areas in County Antrim. His family had already sworn loyalty to the House of Stuart by opposing the MacDonnells of the Isles. The MacDonnell activity was to reap huge rewards in the last years of Elizabeth's reign.

The degree of colonisation in Elizabeth's reign was slight: the 16th century gave but a sign of the events to follow in the 17th century. The Scots of the 16th century were perhaps culturally little different from the Scots of the Isles of 1603. The islanders were soldiers first and colonisers second. The Lowlanders came mainly as settlers and covered a far greater area, and if necessary they became soldiers. Religion divided these two groups. The MacDonnells were Roman Catholics, whilst the vast majority who migrated in the reign of James I were Protestants. There were four principle reasons for the migration to Ulster: first, the union of the two Crowns of England and Ireland brought about a new political situation. Secondly, an interest in colonisation advanced as the 17th century progressed. The idea of settlement in Ulster inspired Protestant England. Thirdly, conditions in Ulster lended themselves to colonisation. Lastly, Scotland increased its population as a colonising country.

To the Tudors the Scots in Ulster represented a threat: their presence in the province stood in the way of fresh colonisation in the 17th century. The Scottish king could not remain aloof from Irish affairs for the MacDonnells formed a link between the two countries. MacDonnell, based in the Isles, found it difficult to be absorbed into Ulster affairs. With the accession of James I of England, Ireland and Scotland were ruled by one man. Scotland now assisted in overawing the Irish into submission. Peace reigned in Ulster with the coming of James, who was a Protestant. At the time of the union of the two Crowns, both the Scottish king and his subjects were keen about planting lands in Ulster. Planting took place in Scotland,

and there was not much difference to the situation prevailing in Ireland. The Isle of Lewis presented the Scots with their first experience of colonisation. An act was passed in 1597 to develop the island for the "King's profit". In 1599, 500-600 settlers set out for the island, many dying as soon as they arrived owing to the harsh conditions that they had to bear. A large number were slaughtered by the native inhabitants three years after they had arrived. James was not discouraged and in 1605 he urged further plantation of the Isles. A new attempt was made to colonise Lewis after the MacDonnells had been suppressed in Kintyre. The traditional owners of the peninsula had been ousted. The MacDonnells were hostile, and much of Kintyre was granted to the Earl of Argyll. Thus the effort to settle Kintyre was not abandoned. The burgh of Campbeltown was founded on the peninsula in 1617. Parliament ratified the grant in 1607. However, the Earl of Argyll became a Roman Catholic and had been declared a traitor. Although settlements in Scotland had been difficult, the Scots nevertheless remained keen about colonisation, not only in Scotland but in Ulster. In Ulster the Scots could settle along with the English, and the two races seem to have initially got on well together.

There were abortive attempts to colonise Ulster in the 1570s even though the English had gained considerable experience of planting Ireland under the Tudors. The plantation of Leix and Offaly had gone under way under Queen Mary, or Bloody Mary, but nothing definite transpired until 1563. In 1584 Queen Elizabeth had put forward the colonisation or plantation of Ulster — a far more ambitious project. There was a Catholic rising in 1598 when most of the English settlers were swept away. However, the Catholic attacks were not sermons, and the English renewed their efforts. James I was preoccupied with Ulster, and the plantations took on a new lease of life during his reign. The plantation of Ulster was based upon English endeavours elsewhere in Ireland.

By the beginning of the 17th century England had looked beyond Ulster and Ireland in order to set up colonies. Sir Humphrey Gilbert had taken up the colonisation of Newfoundland in 1583. In 1600 English merchants incorporated the East India Company, and other mercantile colonies were set up in North America; Virginia standing out and named after the great Queen Elizabeth Tudor. A colony was set up in South America in 1609. However, the motives for planting in the New World were vastly different from those surrounding the plantation of Ulster. Defence was important in Ireland, especially in the north. The English could afford Scots participation in the colonisation of Ulster at a time when England was in need of planters — the possibility of a joint project was now in the offing. The condition of Ireland at the beginning of the 17th century was also instrumental in bringing about the Scots presence. Nearly all of those who wrote about Ulster at this time were foreigners, Scots or otherwise, hostile to the Irish. Britons were encouraged to cross the sea into Ireland. Ulster had green pastures, moors, forests and rivers which could attract the colonisers. Her soil was fertile and rich harvests were yielded. The sea yielded great catches, and Ireland was recorded to be agriculturally as great as anywhere in Europe. The English held the Irish in contempt and looked upon them like the Indians of America. The Scots shared their contempt with England of the Irish or Gaels. Irish institutions in Ulster were a puzzle to the Scots and English who started to govern the land. It was an intolerant age. The Ulster Gaels were regarded as an inferior Catholic race; they needed to receive English civilisation. There were two Ulster institutions that were looked down upon by the English: "gavelkind" and "creating". Gavelkind was the Gaelic system of land distribution and had tended to be divided up amongst a sept: when a member of the Scots died the land was divided up amongst the deceased's family.

There was no security of tenure, and a man had little incentive to improve his plot. In Ulster, people generally moved their cattle into the mountains where they built temporary shelters. The Irish grew oats and barley in temporary enclosures. The English did not like the way the Gaels used the land, so they wanted to deprive the Irish of it. The English considered that a stable form of agriculture would permit closer control by central government. The English knew that the Irish had control of rich pastures which the English and Scots wanted to possess. A province like Ulster cried out for colonisation. Newry was referred to as a "frontier town", but war had decimated her population, and the whole of Ireland had suffered during the Elizabethan wars. In most places waste, decay, famine and pestilence had taken their toll. The Irish wanted to escape from these hardships, and this encouraged the English in their drive for plantation of Gaelic soil. Of all the four Irish provinces, Ulster had fared worst. So followed the depopulation of Ulster. There were reports of sparsity of population. The Lord Deputy, Chichester, said that the population of Ireland had been at its lowest for centuries. In 1600 the English estimated that the Gaels of Ulster could only muster 8,592 fighting men. The total adult population of Ulster was between 25,000 and 40,000, but this was a figure arrived at before the devastating Elizabethan wars, which had brought about famine and plague. The exact number of Ulster people surviving the 16th-century English-versus-Irish campaigns is not clear.

By the beginning of the 17th century there were several factors making for a Scots settlement. The English and Scots Crowns had been united. The Lowland Scots had shown a desire for remote districts, judging by the efforts in Lewis and Kintyre. To plant Ulster effectively the Scots needed money and tenants. If the home country could not supply men and commodities then the Scots efforts were doomed.

Chapter 2

The Scottish Connection

It is a fact that these Scots basically lacked money and resources to carry out an Ulster plantation, for the Irish population was quite large and feared interference from the British mainland. They enjoyed some support from the English, but basically they had a hard task. The fact of the Lewis and Kintyre population pointed to an initial Scots effort in the north of Ireland.

As Scotland entered the 17th century she possessed a firm government, much more so than she had for 100 years. In the previous 100 years from the union of the English and Scots Crowns there had been perpetual internal strife, and there were some foreign invasions.

In Scotland successive minority monarchs gave rise to political unrest, and there were frequent feuds amongst the nobility. In an account written in the 1580s, it was pointed out that the gentry were often as powerful in their own districts as were the great lords in theirs. When King James of Scotland reached his majority there was a strong pressing need for strong central government. For a decade he gradually consolidated his position. At last he gained sufficient power and experience to initiate a number of measures in the outlying districts.

Upon his accession to the English throne James intensified his efforts to establish despotic rule in Scotland. He gradually established a measure of despotic rule. Five months after the union of the Crowns, the Council, on the King's command, established a police force, composed of fifty well-armed horsemen, to enforce the law. The police force was expected to form tight control over the Scottish Lowlands. Its formation represented a new departure in central government. A guard was set up in September 1603, but in 1611 it was reduced in numbers. It was put to good use in the making of arrests and generally enforcing the dictates of the Council. There was also the problem of the lawlessness of the lairds. An act was passed on 5 January 1604 to help combat feuds and showed James's increasing firmness. James tried to banish uncivilised customs, declaring illegal the carrying of pistols and hagbags (portal guns which were supported by tripods). Measures were taken to outlaw the quarrels and violence that accompanied this. In future any laird or lord that was involved in a dispute would have to swear to keep the peace and he would be heavily fined if he did not do so. Some feuds still continued such as those between the Lindsays of Eggell and the Wisharts of Pittarro; the Gordons of Lochinvar and the McClellands; and Lord Stewart of Ochiltree with the Douglases. The Council adopted stern measures to stamp out feuds.

Scotland, by the time of the 17th century, had not known such peace for some time. Sir Thomas Craig, an Englishman, wrote about the year 1605: *There are few in Scotland who had any grievances at all, compared to the numbers in former times.* James introduced justices of the peace into Scotland along the lines of the situation that was prevailing in England. His commands would be carried out from Edinburgh. The size of the Scottish guard was reduced but isolated disorders still continued. James I's accession meant that an era of peace would prevail, and firm government in Scotland would be the rule. When robbery from neighbours turned out to be unprofitable the lairds and outlaws applied themselves to peaceful pursuits. Peace in Scotland, and the organisation of central government at Edinburgh, meant that a concentrated effort of plantation could go ahead in Ulster.

The Scots of the Highlands and the border areas were unruly. The division between Highland and Lowland was an important demarcation line in Scotland's history in the 17th century. The Highlanders spoke Irish and the Lowlanders spoke English, but this is not to say that the Highlanders were regarded by the Lowlanders as foreigners. The men of the borders were regarded as "domestic Scots", but the Crown experienced great opposition in the border areas to central rule. In the borders the political situation was ripe for the growing up of colonisers or planters.

When James was only twenty-one, the Scots parliament attempted to deal with the existing disorder in the more remote regions by passing an act to quell the borders and the Isles.

Border landlords were called upon to provide suitable measures as a guarantee for the good behaviour of those that dwelt on their lands, and any chief or clan that received stolen goods was made liable for their restitution. Their lands harboured outlaws and they permitted them to escape in the face of legislation from central government at London and Edinburgh. In 1599 the government decided that firm measures were essential. By another Act of Parliament thieves would have to pay for their crimes with their lives. In 1603 James packed his bags and left for London, and 1602 saw the culmination of his policies in Scotland. The lairds bound themselves to reform. They had to agree with the policies for the pursuit of fugitives, stamping out the anarchy that had previously obtained.

When James became King of England his position in imposing his authority in Scotland increased substantially. Until 1605 the borders remained under the rule of separate Scottish and English legates, but soon there was a radical change in policies. The entire border region of Scotland and England would come under tight control. The Scots commissioners sometimes worked side by side with their English brethren. The English sent the Grahams, one of the many troublesome clans on the border, to Roscommon. A report was submitted in May 1605 stating the facts of the situation in the border areas. The commission ordered a survey of the number of able-bodied men in these regions. The commissioners would also report superfluous labour on the landlords. Those listed were obliged to serve in the army or navy of either their own or some foreign monarch. Along with firm government would grow population.

By 1606 it was estimated that little could be done to control the rebellious areas. Executions went under way on a smaller scale. A large number of goods had been stolen in the areas of unrest. In 1606 the Earl of Dunbar had assumed overall control of the commission, and he was informed by citizens in the areas of unrest that there was still a large element of trouble. Dunbar had done his best to bring law and order into the rebellious areas, and upon his departure the country relapsed into anarchy — slaughter, rape and crimes commonly committed without risk of punishment. Often criminals received protection from powerful nobles. A petition asked King James I not to listen to reports that the border areas were quiet. Frequent courts were established to mete out stern justice.

The opinions and views of officials were not reliable in recording the condition in the border areas, but the borders eventually obtained a degree of tranquillity. But this did not mean that crime ceased. Seventy-seven charges still faced different members named Johnston (one of the most common names in the borders). The nature of the disorder changed, and disturbances flared from time to time, but on the whole lawlessness was starting to become suppressed, although there were still notorious outlaws. Until Dunbar's death in 1611 severe measures continued. Some died on the gallows and others were banished from the kingdom. However, during 1611 acquittals outnumbered executions. On the whole justice was tempered with mercy. The King visited Scotland in 1617, and the privy council concerned itself little with border affairs. There was, however, a return to disorder and once again border affairs concerned the Council. It was suggested that notorious criminals should be shipped to Virginia, but the border areas were quiet. The "ydle people" contributed a surplus population which could find no place in the civilised order. Enforced emigration and possible death was the punishment for stealing.

There was a surplus population in the border areas. Estimates for the population of Scotland at the beginning of the 17th century number at between 500,000 and one million. The higher proportion lived in the Highlands, which probably had a greater population in the 17th century than in the 21st century. Population density has been estimated at twelve and a half persons per square kilometre, as opposed to forty-four persons in Italy and thirty persons in England and Wales. These figures are open to error and do not take into account the high proportion of Scotland's land which was mountainous or suitable only for rough grazing, but they suggest a very packed population. The weight of Scots population at this time can be derived from many sources. There were first of all the Acts of Parliament passed in the 1590s designed to deal with the growing number of vagrants and beggars. This problem had become worse, even though plague and famine were fairly frequent. There were no hasty government measures based upon unreliable sources. Women were profuse in numbers, and one observer stated that the kingdom itself was overrunning with them. At this time the swarms of people became embarrassing for Edinburgh. Numbers of Scots followed James VI to England, prompting the Scottish Council to issue repeated warnings throughout the region to stem the stream of men and women flowing south. Sometimes the Scots used England as a stepping stone for the Continent. In 1605 the English Council wrote a letter to their opposite numbers in the north sympathising about the Scots position. Scots entered the service of foreign armies, and those who went to the Continent often found themselves in the service of Gustavus Adolphus; others went to France and Holland. Some also went to Poland — no fewer than 30,000 Scottish had settled there.

An excess of population can be looked at from two points of view: there could be a high birth rate, or an economy that cannot absorb a large workforce. It is not known what Scotland's birth rate was. Contemporaries thought it was large, and many others held a similar view. No accurate statistics have come down to us. The Scots economy could not expand at a sufficient rate to absorb the workforce. There was therefore a high unemployment rate. Before James established himself, the unemployed turned to crime. Others had no choice other than to seek work, mainly on the Continent. Only if there were stable conditions in the home country could the capital be raised to plant Ulster.

At the beginning of the 17th century Scotland enjoyed abundant natural resources. There were few natural disasters. In the west, Scotland's rivers, lakes and coastal waters teemed with fish; while the east, particularly in the area between the rivers Tay and Ness, produced an abundant supply of agricultural products. However, Scotland was not as fertile as England, but her Lowlands still produced a soil well suited for agriculture, except perhaps in the south-west. She also possessed a considerable amount of mineral wealth. Lead was mined as well as copper and a little gold. The seas were used for the extraction of salt and there were also large deposits of coal, but she lacked timber. The trees only met the hundredth part of her needs.

Let us look at Scotland's exports in the years between 1611 and 1614: agricultural goods accounted for £300,922 worth of exports or approximately forty-five per cent of the total. Manufacturing in which salt, cloth and linen yarns made up another twenty per cent, whilst minerals, such as coal and lead, and re-exported goods made up the remainder.

Agriculture, of course, was the principal industry: oats formed the staple crop (the natives relied on oats). Barley was the second item, which the Scots used mainly for brewing, though some of it went to make barley bread (consumed mainly by the gentry). Visitors found Scotland well off for cattle and horses, but the animals tended to be smaller than those found in England, caused probably by an inability to feed hay during the winter (straw was the usual winter feed). Those who visited the country remarked that there was no hay. Few enclosures existed throughout Scotland, and only in Moray was there any mention of them. The Scots continued their habit of herding, each man guarding his own beasts no matter how small the numbers. Some think that sheep-raising increased in Scotland after 1603, and this may be correct. However, the East Lothian gentry could have wished to exclude wool imports. About 1621 the Earl of Penrose paid 21,000 marks (about £1,000 pounds) for land to provide pasture for his sheep on the eastern borders, but there is no way of telling if the land previously supported sheep or not.

It is difficult to estimate the efficiency of Scottish agriculture as few comments on the agricultural techniques have survived. The Scots seemed to use similar methods to the English, including the application of lime. The system of land tenure stood out and struck the imagination of observers. It was reckoned that Scotland had an efficient agricultural system. As early as 1521 John Major pointed out that leases were too short. Fearing expulsion at the end of their term, tenants refrained from investing in improvements. Major argued that if landlords granted permanent or, at least, long-term leases, they themselves stood to gain, for the tenants would grow prosperous. The land-tenure system underwent a revolution in the 16th and 17th centuries, and the changes that took place greatly affected the Scots migration into Ulster. There were a great number of dispossessed tenants — at this time they tended to increase the income of the landlords.

There were three main types of tenure: many of the tenants had no security, and it was probably on behalf of these that John Major pleaded. The second category were the so-called kindly tenants who possessed some measure of security, but the exact number and nature of this type of tenure is unknown; it tended to vary according to place and time. It seems to have been based mainly on custom. There were small rents in addition to service to the lord. The third and most secure holding was by "feuing" by which the tenant obtained land in perpetuity in return for an initial payment and a fixed rent. Feuing was practised as early as the 17th century. At first only the Crown, the Church and the burghs let land by these terms on any large scale, and it was only during the 16th and early 17th century that this method of tenure became widespread. Feuing did not necessarily benefit the small tenants and they found the initial cost difficult to meet. Also landlords in the 17th century were reluctant to grant a long-term tenure, for a tenant at will could be threatened with dispossession if he did not take up arms on his lord's behalf, and such support was essential in troubled times. Many customary or "kindly" tenants, although they obtained feu tenure, meant that the original tenants were thrust off the land to make way for feuers. An Act of Parliament in 1567 referred to the expulsion of the common people from their land, and the government had to deal with the problem — three forced off the land became beggars. Feuing undoubtedly increased the number of unemployed in the country. Despite the act, hardship still continued.

So the position of the Scots tenant vis-à-vis his landlord at the beginning of the 17th century was precarious. He was worse off than his English counterpart. So it was realistic that he should leap at the opportunity of coming into possession of land in Ulster.

Scotland was able to produce a food surplus of crops in the early years of the 17th century, and this was aided by good weather. Famine was perhaps uncommon, but visitors after 1600 agreed that her land surplus supplied enough nourishment for her population. One observer stated that *a kingdom so populous as Scotland sold so much bread-corn beyond the seas and yet have more sufficient for themselves.* Between 1611 and 1614 Scotland exported on average grain and grain products (excluding whisky) to the value of £37,177 (Scots) per annum, while grain imported from the Baltic fell from an average of £563 per annum in the 1590s to £211 between 1611 and 1620. Scottish agriculture was therefore weighed heavily in favour of the landlords, leading to an increase of wealth to this class.

The condition of prices at the beginning of the 17th century points to the conclusion that Scotland was enjoying a measure of prosperity, emerging from a period of economic difficulty into relative stability. From 1540 to 1600 Scotland passed through a period of great inflation. Prices of grain, food and household commodities showed a great rise. Prices were controlled but such a move had to be used cautiously. There was a steady increase in prices in the last quarter of the 16th century. Tables from Glasgow, and the records from both Stirling and Kirkcudbright, confirm that inflation was general throughout the country. However these prices only reflect the general inflation in Europe throughout this time. Such occurrences as bad harvests had also to be taken into account. In Scotland the situation was complicated by the debasement of the coinage, the consequence of which was weak central government and civil unrest. In 1570 the Scots pound was worth one fifth of the pound sterling. By 1601 it had dropped to the level of one twelfth of the English pound.

James had established a firm government, but he had to tolerate the debasement of the coinage. During James's reign the movement of Scottish prices can be divided into three sections. The first period, 1603-1609/10, saw a tendency for a rise in prices, but much slower than that which the country was used to. During the middle period, from about 1610-1620, prices remained almost static and even fell at times. The average price of corn between 1610 and 1620 was nearly 4d over the 1609 price. The third period coincided with the disastrous harvests of the early 1620s. Prices soared, but by 1624 they reached some sort of stability, though candles and hay were the exceptions.

Livestock prices are hard to analyse, but valuations at Glasgow showed a slight increase during the first decade of the century and afterwards general stability. There does not seem to be a connection between inflation and the Scots migration to Ulster. Profits were forthcoming. During these years landlords may have been able to build up capital for the eventual Ulster adventure. That Scotland enjoyed economic prosperity in the first half of the 17th century is testified to in the figures for customs receipts (including the import of wine). By the 16th century the government had decided that the collection of customs taxes should be farmed out to private enterprise. During this year the revenue from customs amounted to £76,606 (Scots). In 1616 there was another rise to £150,000 (Scots). A rapid rise in customs receipts points to a period of trade and prosperity, but it is still open to debate what their income was. The records concerning this are more abundant in England than in Scotland. The Earl of Argyll, in 1616-1617, had an income of nearly £22,000 (Scots), and he was one of the largest landowners in the country. The next most wealthy class were the merchants. However, there was a lack of middle-ranking subjects, as in England. Merchants were *poor in wealth and they be few in number*, and one worth £1,000 sterling — or £12,000 (Scots) — was considered very rich. In Edinburgh it was rare for burgesses to reach five figures, and quite a few of them were very prosperous, which is in accordance with contemporary English opinion. Wealth was gauged by estimating the annual income and by the value of a person's property at his death, and the money owed him at death and his debts. However, in the south-west, merchants were less well off than in Edinburgh. George Allason, merchant and burgess, whose free estate was valued at £395 8s 10d (Scots) or nearly £33 sterling was typical of the position. Only rarely do the records show the free state of a merchant's wealth to be much more than £1,000 (Scots). James Bak, who was a bailie of Glasgow and a considerable citizen, left property valued at £8,138 17s 8d (Scots), but this was exceptional.

The Scots merchants prospered in the west, as in the east, in the favourable atmosphere of early 17th century Scotland. The laird of a burgh in Scottish society had never been more powerful, and they challenged the local landed interests. Scotland was mainly an agrarian society. The distinction between town and country is somewhat artificial in the context of the 17th century. Landowners outnumbered merchants and remained firmly in control of government, whether at local level or in privy council.

When commercial enterprise rose it was the landlords rather than the merchants that benefited, as in the case of coal mining. As far as politics was concerned, Glasgow and Dumbarton had to combine in 1633 to prevent the Laird of Greenock having the town erected into a burgh or barony, which meant that it would obtain not only a weekly market and a twice-yearly fair, but also the right to collect customs and tolls.

Industry and commerce had yet to come of age. Few people were involved in trade as a profession. There were those who produced clothing, and there were those who were engaged in the manufacture of armour and drapery. There were a few lawyers clustered round the court at Edinburgh. On the income of articles we have little information. During the period between 1616 and 1626 at Edinburgh, master masons outnumbered the artisan class and could earn as much as 100 shillings (Scots) a week. Ordinary masons made between 60 and 72 shillings. Working all year round they could enjoy an income of from £104 to £260 (Scots) a year. However, the artisans did not benefit from the better economic climate of 1600. Wages in some cases doubled in the improved economic climate between 1580 and 1615. Bread and ale prices increased more than this amount.

In conclusion to this part, two salient features stand out at the beginning of the 17th century. First of all the landlords became more prosperous, but this does not mean that they suddenly became wealthy, for their riches were modest in comparison with English prices. Landlords enjoyed a special place in Scottish society, and this increased the possibility of investments if a suitable venture presented itself. The landlords had been busy at Lewis where they developed coal mines. They competed with royal burghs. As far as migration to Ulster was concerned there was little possibility of landlords and tenants remaining at home when the rich Ulster landscape loomed at the beginning of the 17th century.

Scotland was a Church state. The history of the country is a tale of how the Scots kings tried to obtain a firm grip upon their subjects. They wanted control over things both spiritual and temporal. This trend had started before James had ascended the throne. After James had escaped from captivity in 1583 from the Ruthven lords, parliament passed the so called "Black Acts". These confirmed the episcopal system at the expense of the Presbyterians. It declared that bishops were responsible to the king, not to the general assemblies. James was not old enough to assert his authority by himself. He had to rely upon the Earl of Arran. When the Protestant lords returned to Scotland from England, Arran fled and Melville's party came to the centre of the stage, regaining most of his position he had lost in 1583 and 1584. The period from 1586-1595 was one of Presbyterian ascendancy. Bishops now became subject to the General Assembly. In 1592 parliament passed an act negating the efforts of the Black Acts. The Scots Kirk had come into its own; bishops remained, if only in name. More important was the extension of royal authority retained over the General Assembly. The General

Assembly could now call its own meetings, but the king had to name the date and place of the meetings. If the Crown did not name the date and place, the assembly could not meet legally.

When James became King of England, the bishops had nothing else to do than to sit in parliament. James now argued for the Scots bishops' powers held by the English episcopacy. First he crushed the most extreme Presbyterians. In 1605 nineteen bishops met at Aberdeen, declaring themselves as an assembly without royal consent. James accused some of them of treason. They were convicted and banished. Eight others were condemned to live in the most barbarous part of the kingdom. In 1606 parliament passed an act for the restitution of the estates of the bishops, giving bishops considerable civil authority. James forced his Scottish subjects to accept an ecclesiastical role when they became moderators of Presbyterians and synod. However, there was no great struggle for power between state and Church. The Scots were touched and they endorsed the relationship between clergy and laity. Gilbert Brown, a country priest, was arrested near Dumfries in 1605 and the country people attempted to rescue him from his captors. Nor was there much civility in the attitude towards the clergy. James was not content with changes that took place in the Church, and if he had his way his policies may have succeeded. He failed because he wanted a definite form of worship.

In 1614 James wanted a commission introduced, together with other innovations. He visited Scotland in 1617 to see that these changes were implemented. The Church assembly failed to adopt his proposals, and in response to this the famous Perth assembly met in 1618. James asserted that the Church should be the same in Scotland as in England. After a long delay the Articles of Perth received ratification by the Scottish parliament. Until parliament approved the measures, James's policies affected the Scots very little. The average citizen may not have liked James's policies, with the increase of bishops' power. Only when the Scots were ordered to change their form of worship were they aware of the new religious and political status quo. Even those who were supposed to effect the royal will did so with mixed feelings. Many congregations continued to worship in the manner in which they were accustomed. Ministers had a large degree of freedom between 1606 and 1621, so long as they did not openly oppose James's will. Only at the end of his reign was persecution a problem and a factor in migration. The immigrants in Ulster were to create their own culture, and they regarded themselves as setting up a plantation rather than a colony as was the case in the New World. If effectively used, there would be sufficient talent in Scotland that could be applied to the Ulster plantation. Before this the Scots had to obtain land in the province. James formally made an invitation to the Scots concerning Ulster in 1609, but by this date many of the Lowland Scots had established themselves along the coast of Antrim and Down.

Chapter 3

The Scots in Antrim and Down (1603-10)

News of Queen Elizabeth's death reached Londonderry in 1603, and the governor immediately warned Cecil that Ulster might rise in rebellion. The king could send some Scots into the country. If this policy was not adopted there would be trouble. Many advocated the colonisation of Ulster. Mountjoy, the architect of Hugh O'Neill's defeat, recommended that English and Dutchmen should inhabit Ulster, so that the country should *growe civill*. However, James did little to develop these plans. He said that if Dutchmen were allowed to settle in the area they should pay higher rents than normal customs; and they should be restricted to England and Ireland. If these men were to colonise Ulster they might confront the Crown and try to enjoy a measure of independence from King James and his Church of England court.

A few Scots lived in Tyrone and Donegal even before the main plantation of Ulster began, but there was little opportunity for Scots settlement of this area before 1610. James was reluctant to colonise and plant these counties and there was little land available for settlement in the first few years of James's reign. With the defeat of O'Neill, Irishmen submitted to their new king. With the death of Queen Elizabeth there was no further resistance. O'Neill received a pardon. O'Donnell of Donegal received similar treatment, being given an earldom. But the Crown possessed little land in Tyrone, except for abbey lands in Donegal in October 1603. Such small grants were to lead to a large coming of Scots. To make settlement worthwhile grants had to be made on a large scale. Until the "Flight of the Earls" in 1607, such grants could only be made in counties Antrim and Down. Antrim and Down being close to Scotland, were open for the first arrivals of Lowland Scots.

Antrim may have attracted colonisation from Scotland. In 1590 Perrot had justified the grant that he had made in 1586 to the MacDonnells on the grounds that the local Gaelic chieftain had insufficient people to inhabit the land. During the Tyrone wars England did not spare Antrim any more than the rest of Ulster. A patent in 1604 declared that: *The whole region of the county of Antrim was wasted by rebellion.* The first Scot who had inhabited the area under King James was Sir Randal MacDonnell in 1603. After barely settling himself on the English throne, James instructed the Lord Deputy Mountjoy, to give to MacDonnell all of the Route or North Antrim and the Glens of Antrim. This amounted to 300,000 acres and was completed on 28 May 1603, just before Mountjoy departed for England. The initial grant did not mean that there would be more colonisers or planters. It was simply to acknowledge MacDonnell's control of their land. He now possessed a legal title to the lands he had usurped from the McQuillans of the Route and the petty Gaelic lords of the Glens of Antrim. Now James Fullerton received a grant of Olderfleet Castle at Larne in September 1603. At that time there was no indication of colonisation with British tenants.

The concept of plantation must date back to the initial Scots efforts in 1609. Sir Randal MacDonnell received a re-grant of his lands, the original patent being drawn up in haste owing to the expected departure of the lord deputy. The grant failed to included Rathlin Island, and it obtained a clause requiring forfeiture if the rent was not paid in time. This clause was not stipulated by King James, and would have left MacDonnell under constant threat of losing his lands. In April 1606 Sir Randal MacDonnell was instructed to surrender his original grant for a new one made out rectifying the terms of the old one. The new grant of July 1604 permitted Sir Randal to have the power *to divide the said territories into several precincts — each to contain 2,000 acres at least, and to give different names to each division so that they may become different manors — to set apart 500 acres in each for demesne-lands, and to build a castle or mansion house upon each within several years, to hold courts and appoint seneschals.*

Sir Randal had not requested a re-grant, and as far as we know he made no effort to obtain it. There is also no evidence that the idea came from England. The clause reflects the type of re-grant preferred by Dublin Castle. In embryo these were the plans for the plantation of Ulster. There was as yet no role to be played by the English and Scots. The lands were to be divided into lots between one and two thousand acres and the building of a castle or a large manor house on each of these. This was the situation that existed by the "Flight of the Earls" in 1607. These measures were not novel to Ireland. Similar methods had been used in the ill-fated Munster plantation. The clause in Sir Randal's patent was the first step towards the colonisation of 1600.

Another Scots builder loomed upon the scene: one Hugh Montgomery, sixth Laird of Braidstone in Ayrshire, who had started to cast greedy eyes upon certain parts of County Down. He had been educated at Glasgow University and had led a riotous youth. Like many of his contemporaries he had served in foreign armies, becoming a captain in the French king's

Scottish guards. He narrowly escaped punishment by the Dutch authorities after he had wounded a fellow Scot after feuding with him and pursuing his enemy into Scotland. After returning from Scotland he occupied the Braidstone estate, where he engrossed himself with English affairs. He had a brother, called George, who had previously emigrated to England in about 1584 when he was twenty-two years of age. He had received preferment from Queen Elizabeth to the parsonage of Chedzoy, Somerset. He also took a great interest in the Scottish monarchy.

James made his progress south to England to occupy his new throne in London, and his Scottish courtiers followed him. At London James agreed that Ireland provided great opportunities for his government. Hugh returned to Braidstone to look out for opportunities. Con O'Neill, the principal Irish landowner in North Down, and who owned both Southern and Upper Clandeboye and the Ards, had rebelled against England in 1601. Sir Arthur Chichester was governor of the area and had him imprisoned in Carrickfergus Castle, where he remained even after the queen's death. Montgomery engineered Con O'Neill's escape and flight to Scotland where it was agreed between the two that O'Neill would give half the lands to Montgomery in return for influencing King James to grant him a pardon. Both rode south for London to King James's court. The Laird of Braidstone and his brother set about carrying out Montgomery's part of the bargain, but at this point their plan received a setback. James Hamilton, a former schoolmaster and Scottish agent in Ireland, started to reduce both Con O'Neill's chief and Montgomery's share of the O'Neill lands from one half to a third. The final third he claimed for himself.

It is not known how Hamilton persuaded King James to let him have a share in the planting of O'Neill's lands. No satisfactory answer has been given, but he probably started to interfere in August 1604. O'Neill and Montgomery had arrived at court some time before this, and it was in August that Hamilton, jointly with Montgomery, undertook to put the Irish expenses with England's. Hamilton now concentrated on obtaining land in Ulster. On 6 December 1604 King James issued a letter from Westminster in favour of a London merchant, Thomas Ireland, whereby he would receive lands in Ireland and whereby he would receive an income of £100 per annum. The two Ards fell under colonial jurisdiction. Hamilton was the first Scot to obtain a legal title in Down. The next step in the Scots colonisation of the area was an agreement between Hamilton, Montgomery and Con O'Neill. All the O'Neill lands were granted to Hamilton, who promised to plant the area with the English and Scots. He obtained powers over trading matters; he was also privileged to trade with England and Scotland. Produce was not to be sold locally, and he was forbidden to grant further lands in Ulster except those of Con O'Neill. A survey was to be conducted to determine the extent of the lands concerned.

It was also seen that the seaports were inhabited by the Scots. As far as the other lairds were concerned, they were granted favours by King James, and the Great Ards fell under local rule. At this stage there does not seem to be any great plan for using County Down as the springboard for the colonisation of the rest of Ulster. The scheme that was brought about by Hamilton and Montgomery was one that envisaged the eventual occupation of Gaelic land in the province by British inhabitants. The structure of the Down colonisation was entirely private, but upon this was the authority of King James's government. For the first time in James's reign a grant of Irish land had been made conditional upon the introduction of Scottish and English tenants. Scottish colonisers were now at the same level as Englishmen. James wanted the colonisation of County Down to be successful, and the local Down project was important for the eventual plantation of Ulster.

By 19 June 1605 Hamilton had crossed to Dublin where he presented the plan for colonisation that had been made in London by Sir Arthur Chichester, who by this time had become Lord Deputy of Ireland. Chichester was amazed at the amount of land that had been granted and he explained to Salisbury that if Hamilton had had his way he would have more lands than the great lords of Ireland. Hamilton had received a large grant of land in which he obtained the abbey and priory of Coleraine, Disert (or Kells) and Masserine in Antrim, Newtown, Holywood, Movilla, Black Abbey, Grey Abbey and Bangor in County Down.

By July 1605 Chichester had departed for Ulster in order to settle disputes amongst the numerous landowners. Hamilton probably accompanied him part of the way, and he passed Masserine to Chichester. Thomas Phillips obtained Coleraine, and early in October Hugh Montgomery bought Movilla, Newtown and Grey Abbey for £106 5s. The arrangement between Chichester and Hamilton and its consequences have been thoroughly examined elsewhere. In brief the two men agreed with Thomas Ireland's lawyer to procure property well in excess of the value as specified in the letter. Once a property had been established as belonging to the Crown, Hamilton merely added it to his own personal property. He received no less than five grants between July 1605 and May 1608. Once he had gained a title he would more often than not sell it. It was part of his duty to Chichester or some other servitor. Chichester wished to divide the land given to Hamilton in 1605. Chichester's control of the north enabled him to make up his mind about the Irish, both poor and prosperous. There was however an absence of justices of the peace, and this made good government almost impossible; this deficiency could only be rectified by the planting of Scots and English on Irish lands. Chichester explained that King James could very much make his mark upon the Ulster landscape and he was looked up to by the vast majority of Irishmen, Scots and Irish.

Hamilton had accompanied the lord deputy to the north, and it was probably during the summer that the Scots at first laid sight upon possible land for the plantation of Ulster. Hamilton was impressed by what he saw and a contemporary described the Great Ards as a *champion and fertile land*. South Clandeboye was mostly wooded and had been able to produce forty horses and eighty footmen, but the rebellion in Elizabeth's reign had set matters back. Now there existed a fertile, well-wooded land; however, it was depopulated and wasted. It was to all intents and purposes surrounded by the sea, endowed with numerous harbours and lying near to Scotland, so that the Scots regarded it as very suitable for plantation. Now Hamilton completed his arrangements for the colonisation of County Down.

The survey of Con O'Neill's estate had been completed by November 1605. Hamilton divided two thirds of it equally between Montgomery and the original owners. He obtained the final portion for himself. On 14 February 1606 he received another grant of land as Thomas Ireland's assignee, and once again the grant was as huge. In Antrim it comprised four territories, two granges, one friary, the lands of Castle Toome and the fishing rights of the River Bann from Lough Neagh (the great lake) to the salmon leap. In Down he received the abbey of Comber and a grange, as well as some other scattered townlands near the barony of Dufferin. Hamilton was ordered to build a castle or house in each of the territories on pain of a fine of £30 sterling for every one not built. However, within two months he had disposed of most of the County Antrim land. His affairs in Antrim were legally settled in April 1606, so he now rose to the challenge that presented itself in County Down. He had persuaded his two brothers, Gavan and John, to go to Ireland, for it was in April that they became denizens. Chichester expected more settlers to arrive, and now the flow of Scots into Ulster had started. One observer stated that every day saw a steady stream of emigrants passing over into the province from the Scots homeland.

Among those settlers upon the estates were the Maxwells, the Roses, the Barclays, Mores and Baylies. They obtained short leases, but the settlement seems to have flourished. In July 1607 James wrote to Hamilton that he had decided that Bangor, Coleraine and Belfast should be granted incorporation and other privileges, so the plantation should be encouraged *in our Counties of Downe and Antrim*. Hamilton received a knighthood from King James in 1608 in reward for his services as a planter. We know little about Hamilton's early operations. In his own words he had by 1610 obtained land in the Ards, which had been much sought after by would-be tenants, and we can assume that Hamilton's efforts were a financial success. In 1616 he was so prosperous that he was able to purchase the entire barony of Dufferin. More about Montgomery's plantation in Down has come down to us whilst Hamilton (Sir James) remains in the shadows.

Once the tripartite agreement of April 1605 had been drawn up, Montgomery and Con O'Neill left court. They first of all headed for Edinburgh, then to Braidstone where they stayed for a short while. From here they crossed to Ireland, heading south to Dublin in the autumn. Hamilton sold some of his Church lands to Montgomery and the terms of the tripartite agreement came into effect. Montgomery also received a knighthood in an effort to calm his ambitions to be a large landowner. Sir Hugh Montgomery now returned to Scotland to seek out settlers, which eventually embraced a number of lairds from his own district, often of his own or his wife's family. These people received estates up to the value of 1,000 acres. Sir Hugh, like Chichester, introduced a number of fairly substantial men to help to bear the responsibility of local government and military leadership.

Gentry, artisans, smiths, masons and carpenters migrated from Scotland to Ulster, and they formed the backbone of the plantation. They constructed necessary buildings and were described as wealthy able men. They became small landowners, possessing land of two or four acres apiece. Montgomery gave tenants freehold and parks by lease. "Parks" seems to refer to grazing rights. Under this system Montgomery and his successors managed to increase the rent on park lands from one shilling a year at the beginning of the plantation, to ten shillings an acre by the end of the century; an average yearly increase of ten per cent. Montgomery went about expanding his territory, principally by buying up the lands of the O'Neills that had been left to Con. The colony grew up around Newtown and Grey Abbey. The planters started to arrive in May 1606, and the first task they had was to find settlers. The country was devastated so that not thirty cabins stood upon the land. Montgomery's workmen made temporary repairs to a stump of the old castle in Newtown to provide a home for Sir Hugh and some of his gentry. They also erected cottages for themselves out of sods and trees, using bushes for wattle and rushes for thatch.

A supply of timber and other items was a priority, and this was found locally. Wood used in the construction of the roofs of churches in Grey Abbey and Comber, and the buildings at Newtown and Donaghadeem, came from the Slut Neal region, a heavily wooded area that bordered the River Lagan. The cut timber may have made its way to Belfast. From Belfast the Scots took up settlements overland. Belfast was only about twelve miles from Newtown and other necessities were obtained from Portpatrick and Stranraer. The granting of lands to the Scots in the coastal areas began to pay rich dividends. With a good wind the journey from Portpatrick to Down took less than three hours. During the summer two or three times a week ships would arrive from Scotland, bringing supplies and a constant stream of immigrants. Women as well as men landed upon Ulster shores, and contributed as much as the men to the success of the plantation. During the first few years of the Ards colonisation it was Sir Hugh's wife, Elizabeth, who organised parts of the plantation on her husband's lands. She built watermills and encouraged the manufacture of linen and woollen cloth. Colonisers would come with no money and with only a cow or a few sheep. In return for their labour Elizabeth gave them grazing rights, fodder for the winter, a house and a garden plot. She made the settlement self-sufficient. There were bumper crops during the first few years, and the Scots in the Ards became a prosperous little community. One observer remarked that, *Now everybody minded their trades, the plough and the spade, buildings and setting fruit trees, etc. in orchards and gardens.* The old women spun and the young girls plied their fingers at knitting, so that everyone was busy. There was no strife, contention, or Scottish or Irish feuds to disturb the tranquillity of those times.

Meanwhile in County Antrim the Gaelic population fell under the Scots hammer. There were grave risks involved in establishing a colony. Hamilton's ambition, it has been shown, did not apply to County Down only but extended to Antrim as well. Upon his arrival in Ulster he became embroiled in a dispute with Sir Randal MacDonnell over the fishing rights on the River Bann. Sir Randal's original grant included fishing rights on his lands but it excluded those on three quarters of the River Bann, and this implied that he had obtained fishing rights on a quarter of the river. In February 1606, James Hamilton acquired the fishing rights from Lough Neagh to the salmon leap. Thomas Ireland's assignees, the MacDonnells, did not raise an objection to this and understood that his share was from the leap to the sea. Upon returning from the trip to England where he had been pleading for a reduction in his rent, he found the situation transformed. On 2 March 1606, one John Wakeman had received a grant of the Bann fisheries from the leap to the sea. On the next day he sold his rights to John Hamilton. Sir Randal expressed his feelings in a letter to Salisbury: he claimed that Hamilton had deprived him of his fishing rights on the River Bann, which had constituted his main source of income.

The MacDonnells' "little" portion was 300,000 acres, and an inquiry into Sir Randal's patent showed that Hamilton did no more than was common in Ireland at this time. There seems to have been an attempt to separate the MacDonnell chiefs from their lands. Sir Thomas Phillips reported adversely about Sir Randal MacDonnell, and he tried to discredit the MacDonnell chief, reporting that he had caused a riot over its ownership. This report turned out to be false. The dispute raged on until the City of London obtained the rights at issue. After a long battle Hamilton won his case, and he had been in league with Sir Arthur Chichester, the future deputy. He had presided over the court that delivered the verdict. Chichester had a great reason to dislike Hamilton, for in 1597 James MacDonnell had killed Sir Arthur's brother, Sir John Chichester. When he became lord deputy he was bent on victimising the MacDonnells. The man appointed to supervise matters over the MacDonnell clan was Captain Thomas Phillips. Chichester purchased from Hamilton the Bann fisheries from Lough Neagh to the salmon leap on 10 April 1660 — that part which was disputed between Hamilton and MacDonnell was reconciled on 14 May 1606.

A letter dated 14 June, a month after the transaction, stated that peaceful conditions had come about in Antrim by granting land from the former Irish chiefs to the British. In the Route or North Antrim and the Glens of Antrim, without regard to the native inhabitants the locals were now treated as slaves. The letter went on to say that Sir Randal's efforts to have his rent reduced had already come to the attention of King James I. Chichester ruled that most of the land should remain in MacDonnell's hands. Some of the MacDonnells' lands were forfeited to the Crown. By this the entire coast from the River Bann estuary to Dublin would be intensively planted and rendered profitable to King James.

Chichester knew that the MacDonnells wanted a reduction in their rent, and he brought an agent to supervise the Scottish clans. Sir Randal was accused of not looking after his tenants. One Englishman reported that the families living in the Glynns *are most desirous to live under the Scots, since they do better with them, and less spoiled than the true Irish.* Later on in the summer the deputy heard more adverse reports about Sir Randal MacDonnell. He was said to be involved in plots against the lord deputy and that he had access to the king. Chichester wrote a letter to Salisbury in which he remarked that MacDonnell was a vicious person not to be trusted in the north. The changes this time were no more reliable than those in the first letter. One must ask the question of who sent the information about the Scot to the deputy. It is perhaps likely that Phillips, whose view was prejudiced, may have provided the information. The case against Sir Randal MacDonnell was never proven. Moreover the deputy's ownership of many lands in Antrim, and his purchase of the fishing rights which Randal claimed, suggest that his abuse of the Scots and his attempt to curtail the size of the MacDonnell estates were motivated as much by private as by public concern.

The constant bickering about what lands were available and planted in Antrim were to take their toll. Little information about the conditions in Antrim during the first half of the 17th century are extant. These disputes must have had an adverse effect on the lands to be colonised and were also bad for the morale of the planters. Violence arose out of the uncertainties regarding the land. The disputes had been intense in 1606, and there were robberies and stealing along the banks of the River Bann. Not all the disturbances along the Bann were carried out by the MacDonnells and their feuds with their neighbours. But MacDonnell, in 1606, complained that his tenants were being terrorised by Phillips, who forced them to flee from their homes. The introduction of the plantation along the banks of the Bann added fuel to the already existing state of unrest.

Despite Sir Randal MacDonnell's clash with authority (with Hamilton and the English officials), despite attempts to chase him off his portion of lands, some emigration into his lands in Ulster by the Lowland Scots came about before 1610. The first to arrive were the Lowlanders who had been planted in Kintyre by the Earl of Argyll, but they were forced to flee in 1607 from the fury of Angus MacDonnell of Dunyveg, the former owner of the Kintyre peninsula. Other Scots made their way into Antrim from Kintyre. In May 1608 the Irish Council received instructions that Sir Randal MacDonnell would make denizens out of those Scots who wished to inhabit his lands so long as they were not Islanders or Highlanders.

We know very little about the Scots portion in the Route and the Glens of Antrim. It is impossible to estimate the extent of the colonisation and movements of Scots in the county, nor is it possible to ascertain the success of the Scots colonisation. It is certain that the Scots efforts in County Down provided the Scots of Antrim with a spur to colonise the entire county. Also, Sir Randal would benefit from the emigration and he would increase his revenues from the estates. He could repair his relations with Dublin and maintain them with London. In the summer of 1607, after the Scots had visited the court, Chichester received orders to make freeholders on his lands on English terms *as Sir Hugh Montgomery and other of our farmers in those parts doe.* Sir Randal was now open to no more criticism from the deputy and other officials. He continued to ask for a reduction of his rent, and this point was settled to his satisfaction in 1610. He surrendered 2,000 acres to the Crown to help carry out the main plantation scheme, and his military operations were also abated. Rent for the remainder of his lands was reduced by half. A new tranquillity of relations between MacDonnell and the English officials in Ireland grew up, and MacDonnell could develop his estates without interference from Dublin.

Until 1610 Coleraine was part of County Antrim. It is useful to note that the transference of Coleraine from Hamilton to Phillips was the plan to develop a settlement at this town. Phillips fulfilled the trust placed in him. The Bann emptied into the Atlantic Ocean at Coleraine. Forty to sixty barks and boats entered the Bann every year. He granted merchants a four-year period of freedom of customs, thus encouraging trade.

A strong Scots community soon grew up as they were working men. It is not clear whether the influx of Scots was due to traders, who stayed only a short while, or to permanent settlers. There was thus great intercourse between Coleraine and Scotland, which led to a Scots settlement in the town. The Scots settlement at Coleraine was relatively small, covering some of Sir Randal MacDonnell's trade, and was reminiscent of the colonisation of parts of County Down. The Scots settlement at Antrim was carried out by the Lowland Scots and was more intense than in the days of Queen Elizabeth. For generations the Scots in Antrim had been warlike Islanders. At the beginning of James I's reign the MacDonnells were discouraging the Lowland Scots from settling on land in Antrim. The Scots revolutionised the colonisation situation in County Antrim. The settlement of Down and Antrim were part of James I's great plan for colonisation in Ulster, and the rule of law would obtain in the north. A greater influx of

Scots was to come. There was however a difference between the Scots colonisation in Antrim and that in County Down. In Antrim the colonisation was perceived without plan. There was no compulsion to introduce settlers as in Hamilton's grant in 1606. Only the construction of buildings was undertaken. However, the colonisation was a patchwork. The lord deputy criticised Sir Randal MacDonnell. The British wanted to thoroughly colonise Antrim with gentry. The British were to forfeit the Irish dwellings and acted as a stabilising force in Ulster. The entire Route and the Glens of Antrim were granted to Sir Randal and had to some extent interrupted the colonisation process. But the Scots from 1606 onwards could not all settle in one plot. In Antrim there remained numerous Irish and Islanders. The Lowland Scots tended to remain with the other settlers.

In Down the opposite situation obtained. The estates of Montgomery and Hamilton had been put aside: the Scots tended to settle on one area which was to be converted into a Scottish "Pale". No emphasis was placed upon building fortification. Parts of the Ards and South Clandeboye suffered from depopulation while this was not to prevail in County Antrim. Orders came from Dublin that fortifications should be erected in both Sir Randal's and Hamilton's grants. The Scots colonisation of Down, in comparison with that in Antrim, was carried out without much consultation with King James. It was the policy of the Dublin government to leave the bulk of the population in Irish hands. Fortifications were to be symbols of British power. Chichester wished to avoid bad feelings between the British colonisers and the Irish, which might lead to disorder or a small-scale revolution. Intense colonisation of the land in Antrim would consolidate British power and divide the Irish.

Chapter 4

A View to a Conquest

A lot has been written about the "Flight of the Earls" in 1607 that took place from the shores of Lough Swilley in north-east Donegal, which was part of Ulster. The planting of the counties east of counties Antrim and Down went forth. Even before the plantation of Ulster some Scots lived in the area. New Scots-Irish planted the Strabane area in County Tyrone. A large settlement had taken place ever since Agnes Campbell had brought over some 1,000 men at the time of her marriage to Turlough Luineach in 1569. At the beginning of the 17th century the settlement consisted of some sixty to eighty families and still retained a Scots identity.

James I had been on the throne of England for seven years. Western Ulster was extensively planted under the auspices of George Montgomery and he was raised to the Deanery of Norwich, a reward for intelligence work he and his brother had organised. In 1605 measures were taken to Protestantise the Irish. When James was rewarding Montgomery's activities in the lands of Down, the king ordered his promotion to the bishopric of Derry, Raphoe and Clogher, these grants being received on 15 June 1605. However, he had not travelled to Ireland until the autumn of the following year. Now Montgomery studied the lands that the Church might obtain. Montgomery's wife helped him in his efforts at plantation, and she mentioned that leases were available. Tenants began to arrive in 1607. The bishops issued proclamations at Glasgow, Ayr, Irvine, Greenock and other south-western ports of Scotland, particularly Braidstone where his brother had a large estate. He declared that he would lease Church lands on easy terms over the next three years; these measures affected a number of Scots in Donegal.

About the same time that Montgomery was carrying out his activities, a few other Scots were moving into Derry and Lifford. Lord Deputy Chichester toured the north in 1605, and he recommended the settlement of many townlands to Anglo-Scottish settlements: he said that Phillips should undertake a plantation at Coleraine, still in 1605 part of County

Antrim. Now Sir Henry Docwra had made his proposals two years before recommending plantation of the rich lands around Down and in Antrim/ Tyrone generally. Derry was granted to the City of London in 1610, and the former residents had to be compensated. Amongst those who received compensation were five or six men — about one fifth of the total. Their names recorded the inhabitants of south-west Scotland, such as Boyd, Petterson and Wray. Few were to remain well off as a result of compensation.

In Lifford there was an impressive Scots presence, making up ten to fifteen per cent by 1610. Lifford had only one house in 1607 and in the same year Sir Richard Hansard, an English servitor, took up the task of turning it into a stronghold. By July 1611 the town boasted sixty houses, comprising English, Scots and Irish. The town was well furnished. In 1612 the townsfolk sent a letter to the lord deputy, upon which appeared many names of the thirteen burgesses. At least two had Scottish names, and of the twenty-nine freemen listed, three were stated to be specifically Scots, and at least two other names on the letter were common names in Scotland.

The Scots of Derry and Lifford had little say in the scheme for plantation that was sent forward. They helped to build the British bases which were part of Chichester's plan for the north. Scots were leaving for Ulster without official approval. Those that had settled under Bishop Montgomery have left few traces behind them. No mention is made of them apart from pieces appearing in the Montgomery manuscripts. However, Montgomery had been remembered in Ulster — not specifically for the plantation scheme, but for the pressure he put on the Earl of Tyrone and Red Hugh O'Donnell to vacate lands in the north.

On 4 September 1607 the earls of Tyrone and Tryconnell, along with about sixty friends, relatives and followers, took ship from Rathmullen on the banks of Lough Swilley. Their purpose was to go into exile. This flight was no doubt a result of the English pressure on the northern earls. The noblemen complained at the treatment meted out to them. Tyrone resented English pressures that were put upon his estates; in this respect George Montgomery posed the greatest threat. There were quarrels between Montgomery and Tyrone, the latter owning Church land. As in England, wealth of the monasteries had been confiscated. Tyrone finally submitted in 1603, and O'Neill's right to levy rent in the north had to be questioned. Tyrone sued for peace, and English power became established in the area. Servitors quickly stepped in to confiscate lands and the monastic lands. The amount of land — until the advent of Montgomery — was quite small.

When Montgomery became bishop of the three northern sees, he declared that the relative lands belonged to the Church, not the Crown. The land had been escheated as a result of their being no bishop to defend the Church's interests. At length Montgomery laid claim to what amounted to half of County Tyrone.

Montgomery used the Gaelic or Brehon laws in accordance with his own interests. All Church land in Ireland was termon or herenagh land, the distinction between the two was that the former possessed certain privileges, such as salting, denied to the termon tenants. The tempore lord gave the monasteries a number of free duties. With the arrival of the bishops, the septs paid rent to the Church, and they helped to maintain the churches and provided for hospitality and other duties. They were not movable by the local bishops and their position was somewhat exceptional by the Gaelic laws. The bishops' claim had little or no validity in law.

About six months after the O'Neill dispute Lord Deputy Chichester claimed that the Church was wanting too much land. Chichester was determined that Tyrone should have none of the Church lands. Tyrone had complained vis-à-vis the Church land that he was becoming victimised and pushed off his lands by the English lord deputy. It was difficult to determine what was Church land, and so the issue remained open. In order to end the dispute, Tyrone proposed the following May that Montgomery had an eye for his lands. Montgomery was determined that the case should not reach the courts. He argued that the bishops must be true landlords. He put aside the ancient Irish custom as being incompatible and said it had grown up in "lawless times", when the O'Neills were troubling the Church. He was against a trial, for the people were for the O'Neills. If Tyrone received a title then the see of Londonderry would virtually disappear. The king would instruct the O'Neills to dispute the case. James was all for having a strong Protestant Church in Ireland, and said that it should receive sufficient land in order that it should flourish.

The dispute with O'Neill was not the only aspect of the dispute with Montgomery. The earl had fallen out with one of his vassals, Sir Connell O'Cahan. He was summoned to London to appear before King James. He believed that he might be in danger of going to jail, so he took flight. Montgomery was pulling his influences all the time with James. He denied that he had stirred up O'Cahan, and he listened to complaints from tenants about how landlords treated him. O'Neill by now had definitely decided upon flight. The nationality of Tyrone's persecutor has to be taken into account. Montgomery was the only Scot with an Irish bishop. His other colleagues regarded the position of the Church in a sluggish manner. He was persistent in his efforts to obtain endowments for his sees and often shocked the lord deputy, who rebuked him for having more care for the Church's material possession than its spiritual needs.

As has been pointed out, King James I was not at first keen about planting many lands in Ulster, but after four or five years he came to see the advantages of Ulster plantation. Keeping law and order in Ulster was a major task. Lord Deputy Chichester had toured the north in 1605. It was decided to spend money in Ulster, and this exceeded what the government spent on the Tyrone wars. There was also a strategic problem: Ulster could not be left to go its own way, for a disorganised Ulster was a threat to England. A French visitor to England said that Ireland was England's Achilles heel. The adversary of England could easily take over a disorganised Ulster or Ireland and use it for the conquest of the Stuart realm. A strong presence in Ulster would lead to an extension of England's power in Ireland. Sir Francis Bacon declared that the English presence in Ulster would include the colonisation of the wilder parts of Scotland and the annexation of the Low Countries.

In the early 17th century strategic considerations could hardly be separated from religious issues. A third reason for the colonisation of Ulster was that Ireland should become part of the Protestant-dominated European system. King James declared to Chichester some two years after setting up the plantation that the state Church had to have precedence, and that the Dublin government was to be for Ulster's advantage. Christian principles held strong in Ulster, more so than in the rest of Ireland. King James seldom did anything that he did not like doing and he was of the view that he might have planted in the north no matter what happened. He regarded the plantation of Ulster as a missionary endeavour and he became more and more for it as his reign proceeded. He regarded the Gaels of Ulster as being barbarous, and to evangelise them was part of the mission of his reign. James wanted to be remembered for his role in the plantation of the north of Ireland.

The enthusiasm for the plantation was with James before the "Flight of the Earls" in 1607. The reorganisation of Cavan was being considered, and it was reputed that King James was very favourable to the idea. Plantation meant the changing of Irish tenure to English, with the introduction of non-Irish tenants being kept to a minimum. Plantation was to be confined to Church lands and there seemed to be an attempt to oust the original Gaels from the land. After the "Flight of the Earls" attitudes changed, so that the situation in County Down was considered for colonisation along with County Cavan. The two earls, intent upon flight, had been accompanied by Maguire, owner of half of Fermanagh. The fugitives were then convicted of treason and much of their lands in Tyrone and Donegal were opened for plantation. To this land could be added County Cavan, a county escheated to the Crown in the following year. Almost immediately after the "Flight of the Earls", the English started to plant their lands.

The Scots also participated in the colonisation, but the planters could not make up their minds on the nature of the plantation. On 17 September, just thirteen days after the flight of Tyrone, Chichester outlined proposals for the planting of the estates. He favoured the idea of most of the land being granted in small lots to the Irish freeholders, with the remainder going to servitors who would plant settlers from both England and Scotland. The plan was close to what had happened in County Antrim. He also considered the possibility of driving the Gaels from Tyrone and Tryconnell (Donegal), making them resettle in the wastelands, which implies that all of Tyrone and Donegal would be turned over to the colonisers. The privy council approved Chichester's plan. They said that the plantation should proceed quickly and stressed that the colonisers should be a mixture of English, Irish and Scots, with the English servitors having first choice of the lands. From this date the Scots had become serious colonisers in the Tyrone and Donegal lands. Chichester was the first to propose granting of lands to the Scots. It was not proposed to combine the two nationalities; Scots and English together. The role that the Scots should play remained secondary. He approved of the Scots forming undertenants. The Scots had been successful in Antrim and Down and this was a good indication that they would effectively colonise Tyrone and Tryconnell. However, the lord deputy had had a dim view of the Scots and the Irish for he said that they were *weaklynes sucking at Englang*. The planting of parts of Ulster would relieve the pressure on England.

Subsequent events in Ulster were to prove the lord deputy wrong. Within three months the Irish administration was having to ask Scotland for support to aid his powers. In April 1608 the land of Inishowen burst into open rebellion, for O'Doherty was at odds with Sir George Paulet, the Governor of Londonderry. Culmore Fort was taken on the 18th and Londonderry sacked the next day. O'Doherty went on to burn Strabane, causing the town's inhabitants to flee to Lifford. Those in authority, whether in Ulster or elsewhere, realised that Scotland possessed a lot of force which could defeat a rising in the north of Ireland as the result of effective colonisation. Six days after the Ulster insurrection began, Chichester wrote to the Scottish Council informing them of rebellion and that it could spread to parts of Scotland, namely the Western Isles. News of the rebellion reached Edinburgh, whereupon the Council acted. The situation at Londonderry was getting out of hand, and Edinburgh asked the Scottish government for five hundred men and two ships to be sent from Scotland.

London responded to the crisis more cautiously. Two hundred Scots were levied and sent to Ulster right away. They stopped at Ayr on 20 June, and the little Scots force set sail for Carrickfergus under command of captains Crawford and Stewart. This was the first time in history that the English used a Scots force to contain rebellion beyond her borders. Two companies landed in Ulster, one of them remaining in Carrickfergus, whilst the other went to join the lord deputy at Dungannon in County Tyrone. They arrived too late to crush the rebellion which had collapsed by the end of June. The question now arose of what Chichester should do with the rebels. The Scots companies received higher wages than other troops in Ireland. Chichester was not able to pay the troops so he was unsure whether he could persuade them to remain in the country. In mid-July the Scottish Council suggested that for having helped in the Ulster emergency the force should in turn be ready to help in a primitive expedition to the Isles. The lord deputy thanked the Scots for their prompt aid and agreed to send two hundred men to help in the Isles, to be used only in a tight situation. At this time an invasion of Ireland was threatening from abroad. The Scots, upon Chichester's proposal, agreed to remain in Ulster on English rates of pay.

By mid-September there was no longer a foreign threat, and the English government released the Scots from their obligations in Ulster. James hoped that the Irish would be overawed and that the rest of them would marvel at the effectiveness of the union. King James had no intention of paying his Irish troops better than his English ones. There were those that volunteered to remain at the standard rate of pay. Those not willing to escape the inferior rates were disbanded in small lots to assure the Irish that the English were full of good intentions. Few Scots troops left Ireland. Both captains of the Ulster force received shares in the escheated lands as servitors. In May 1610 orders went out to give Captain Stewart his proportion, and it was added that he should retain his company in Ulster until the king gave orders to the contrary. Most remained along with their commanders to provide a source from which the Scots landlords might later obtain tenants.

O'Doherty's rebellion led the English to extend the area of colonisation. County Coleraine became part of the disinherited lands. Although he had never been convicted of any crime, the English regarded Sir Donnell O'Cahan as being involved in the rebellion and sent him to the Tower of London. All the lands held by the rebel Shane O'Neill in 1569 were escheated to the Crown. Ards and Clandeboye in County Down were confiscated from Con O'Neill. Other lands in Ulster, in the Fews, in Armagh, were incorporated into the plantation scheme. The Crown now had at its disposal extensive lands in Tyrone, Donegal, Coleraine, Armagh, Cavan and Fermanagh.

Well before the O'Doherty rebellion the Crown was planning its plantation scheme in Ulster. Sir John Davies had secured Tyrone's and O'Donnell's indictment early in 1607, so that James could go ahead with English designs. In the plan the Crown maintained a subsidiary portion. Only in Tyrone did the deputy set up extensive British colonisation. Planting would prove expensive, and he considered undertakers should have their lands free of rent for several years. Chichester now proposed that he should leave for the north to carry out the plantation scheme. The commissioners were delayed by the rebellion in Ulster, but they set out north on 5 July from Dublin. The survey was completed by September, and now Chichester informed the law lords of his intentions in Ulster. In Cavan he suggested that only one barony be granted to the British. He saw the perils of depriving the Irish of their homes. He was not of the view, as others were, that the whole of Ulster should be colonised by the British. The privy council in England did not commit itself to a definite plan of action, but there were also those that held different views.

The main fear was that the colonised would outnumber the colonisers *as weeds overgrow the good corn*. By mid-October Chichester realised that the British settlers, more particularly the Scots, were to occupy large tracts of land that were deemed as necessary. Not only would tenants be brought from Scotland as was proposed, but some of the undertakers as well. Chichester was of the opinion that if large numbers of Scots colonised Ulster there would be grounds for trouble in the future. He was of the opinion that the Irish settlers should remain with their lands.

The English government drew up a commission to apportion the land and draw up conditions of settlement. The Scots that sat upon the commission were Sir James Fullerton, who would speak on behalf of the Scots, and George Montgomery, who would defend the interests of the Scots of the Church. The commission faced its first task on 29 November, when it was proposed to plant County Tyrone. A month later the commission issued a plan. This included Scots, both as tenants and undertakers. New towns were to be created and artisans became part of the colonisation process. However, it was expected that the Scots would settle on the land rather than patronise the towns.

The Council liked Chichester's plan, and it was now proposed that the colonisation should extend to the other escheated counties. The plantation formed part of Chichester's overall plan for Ulster. Church lands were to be extended and land was also partitioned into towns. The Irish landlords remained loyal to the English, together with the Scottish undertakers and servitors. At Londonderry the Church was of the opinion that termon lands belonged rightfully to the Church, but this was overruled. James decided to give these lands to the Church either as bishops' lands or as glebes. The Irish still received a generous portion of land. About 79,000 acres were assigned to the Church and 155,000 set aside for division between Scots and English. In one account Chichester's wishes were carried out, for he desired to see the land distributed only amongst Irishmen. Connor Roe Maguire had been promised three baronies in Fermanagh, amounting to about 12,000 acres, but he was not allowed to keep all this territory. He was forced to sell up under pressure from the planters, and settlements were made in his territory. If the scheme had been put into effect the Scots would have obtained land in Fermanagh. At this moment a pamphlet was published specifying the conditions to be observed by the planters.

The estates or proportions of the undertakers were to be of three sizes — 1,000, 1,500, and 2,000 acres, but these acres did not include rough ground. The planter was assigned a lot and the Crown granted it to him — the first two years of rent being free. Tenure was to depend on the size of the lot. Undertakers with 2,000 or 1,500 acres were to hold their land in onerous knight's service. If the heir was a minor the Crown had a right to ownership. Only the small lots were to be held in common socage, which was exempt from this burden. Building obligations depended upon the amount of land granted. All lots had to have their buildings, but the large ones had to have a castle with a bawn or court surrounding it, while the lesser ones had to have a stone or brick house with a bawn. All undertakers had to take the oath of supremacy, be resident for five years themselves, and have settled a competent number of English or Scots tenants. The plantation had to undertake not to give any land to the Gaels, and they had to be in Ireland ready to receive further instructions by Midsummer's Day (24 June 1609).

At length the Scots, by late March 1609, received official notification of their inclusion in the planting scheme. Sir Alexander Hay, the Scots Secretary wrote to his Council informing them of the plans for colonisation. This took place on the 19th of the same month. It was proposed that the Scots should play a role. James declared that Ulster should be planted in lots *so that the hole people of the one nation should not be cast to ether all in one place.* This plan prevented Ulster from being dominated by large landowners. 2,000 acres meant an area of two square miles, and a number of castles were to be built. The Scots were informed that they did not have to settle in Ulster until May 1610.

Chichester now completed a criticism of the plans and wrote his letter to the Council in Edinburgh. He objected to the knight's service tenure. He opposed the plot system, whereby a planter was given a portion. However, the whole scheme was postponed for a year, during which time a more accurate survey took place. A change was made in the distribution of the proportions in Ulster, and all the escheated counties were divided into portions, some of which were set aside for Scots colonisation and others for different sorts of planters. Large landowners were to cast lots for the precincts and each large undertaker was to be responsible for the distribution of land within his allotted grounds. No more than two acres were allotted to the Scots in any single county. The counties usually contained five or more precincts, so this meant that there would be a revised scheme of distribution, permitting friends to become neighbours. James was all for the integration of the Scots with the English. Another commission was now set up.

In July 1609 the commission left Dublin for Ulster. By 10 August Sir John Davies was writing to Salisbury from a camp near the Blackwater River about methods used by the surveyors. There were five baronies in Armagh, and a surveyor was sent to each barony. They were accompanied by some of the Gaels who were friendly to the British regime. Upon their return to camp the surveyors discussed the situation. Now, in February, Sir Josias Bodley, one of the chief surveyors, endorsed the British methods. They had also discovered many thousands of acres missed by the previous survey. Bodley's survey remained much to be desired. By 1622 about 14,396 acres had been included in the survey. This meant penalties for the colonisers. There were also questions of who should possess the land. By 30 September the commissioners had finished the circuit of the north, although it took a further five months before the survey was completed. The deputy issued a series of reflections upon the project. He objected to the terms, but he had made a number of additional recommendations. He stressed that the colonisations would fail if the planters were not capable. Thus persons of rank were invited to participate. The wealthy would then be able to help the less wealthy planters. He recommended that the time allotted for building castles be extended to four years, from two as previously allowed. He maintained that those in personal residence by the undertakers would be self-defeating, as no one of any importance would be willing to submit to such virtual exile for so long. Lastly he recommended that freedom of rent should be extended from two to three years; and for a further three year period, in which only half the rent should be exacted.

Sometimes the deputy's advice was ignored, but the final set of conditions published in April record his suggestions. The size of the lots were to remain unchanged. The chief undertakers would remain with their 3,000 acres each. Wood and bog land were not to be counted in the calculation of the acreage assigned. The knight's service tenure was to be abandoned, all lands were granted in free and common socage. The rent-free period was also extended from two to four years. The time allowed for building was extended from two to three and a half years. All bawns were to be built within one month of the arrival of the colonisers.

The tenants of course were affected by the law. The first set of laws required a competent number to be settled, but the laws of 1610 were far more specific. Twenty-four able-bodied Scots or English over the age of eighteen were to be planted on estates of 1,000 acres. These were to come from the different families; one third of them had to be there by 1 May 1611, and the last third by 1 November. Two of the families were to be made freeholders of 120 acres of land each. Three more were to receive leases, whilst the remainder was made up of artificers or cottagers. It was the obligation of the undertakers to house these families close to the fortifications.

The timetable was changed in accordance with the new conditions. All the undertakers were supposed to be in Ulster by 24 June, and they were expected to settle in lots by 30 September. The conditions remained very much as before. Undertakers had the power to create manors and hold courts twice a year. They were to have use of timber for two years, regardless if it grew on their own land. They could export goods out of Ireland for seven years and import other necessities like food. They could not import merchandise. They were obliged to arm their tenants, who had to be ready to muster twice a year. Everyone had to take the oath of supremacy. Irish could not hold the land. All undertakers had to put up a bond of good surety, which might by forfeited for failure to carry out the conditions.

The conditions were published in 1610; before this a little table of escheated lands was drawn up, which earmarked the lands to be occupied by the Scots. As before they were to receive territory in counties Armagh, Cavan, Donegal and Tyrone. The Scots settlement was to be extended into County Fermanagh, but they had been excluded from Londonderry, a county newly created out of County Coleraine and part of County Tyrone. This was to be granted to the City of London for settlement by the numerous companies. The Scots in all received 81,000 acres distributed between the precincts, two in each county, except Armagh where only one precinct was settled by the Scots. There were mistakes in the surveying procedure: wood and bog land was omitted from the survey, but the area overall was extensively colonised. The Scots grew rich upon the colonised lands. When the Scots were asked to colonise Ulster, it was like acquiring two additional counties in Scotland. They had four years to carry out their plan.

The inclusion of Scots in James's plans for the north of Ireland had substantially developed since the initial settlement in counties Antrim and Down, which had been a foothold for the eventual plantation of Ulster in the western counties. Chichester based his plan for the north upon the Scots presence in Antrim and Down, which had existed from ancient and medieval times. The building classes resembled those in County Antrim. Sir James Hamilton, who knew most about the government's plans in Ulster, had become very concerned about the plantation in the north. He was in England in October 1609, and again in May 1610. He at length bought land in County Cavan, and he bequeathed land to some of his friends. Hamilton realised that there would be great difficulty in settling the Scots on Irish soil, especially in Ulster. The success of plans in the north relied upon the nature of the colonisers. Failure might easily come about.

Chapter 5

The Undertakers

The appointing of the Scottish undertakers had undergone a long period of evolution similar to that which formed the status quo on the land. It had been Sir Alexander Hay who had informed the Scottish chancellor that to him and the rest of the Council had fallen the responsibility of the Scottish undertakers. Before this all matter relating to the plantation scheme had been made in England or Ireland. The Scots might be able to form their own plan of action. Hay pointed out that if too few Scots applied, then Scotland's reputation might suffer. Englishmen would say that the Scots were too poor to participate in the scheme. If any of the conditions were too severe, he promised to take up the matter with King James. However, he declared that there would be no reduction of rent. Not all of the Scots had to make their applications at Edinburgh; they could apply to London, but they had to find sureties in Scotland. Hay realised that it would be burdensome to transport tenants and cattle over to Ulster and to provide the colonisers with supplies until they became independent. The Scots had an advantage over England for they were too close to the coast of northern Ireland. The Scottish Council issued a proclamation on 28 March announcing the plantation and the intention of the king (for James as a Scotsman loved the Ulster and Scottish colonisers). All those interested in going were invited to apply to the privy council, whereupon they would be provided with the details concerning the colonisation of Ulster.

In March 1609 two Scots had put their names down for the proposed colonisation of the province. These were James's cousins, the Duke of Lennox and Lord Aubigny. They wanted to undertake the settlement of part of Coleraine, which at this stage, in 1609, had not yet been assigned to the City of London. It is not known at what date the request was made, but it was probably before Hay's letter reached Scotland. Neither of them found surety in Scotland as they were required to do. Another Scot now put his name forward for a place in the escheated territories. Robert Hamilton of Stonehaus, Lanarkshire, received a letter from the king on 6

41

June, promising him land in County Armagh. He had to conform to all the traditions. He was enrolled by the Scottish Council for 2,000 acres on 13 July; he had provided a bond of £400, another Hamilton serving as his cautioner.

By now the Scottish Council was receiving requests from Scots living at home. The first of these were enrolled on 13 June, and from that date until the summer applications flowed in. By 30 July a list of names had reached the Scottish Secretary from Scotland. Hay wrote to Lord Salisbury from Bewlie, Hampshire, saying that many Scots had promised sureties and that they wished to obtain grants. The total areas they requested came to 75,000 acres. The roll sent to Hay has not survived, but the names can be deduced. Between 13 June and 20 July the Scottish Council had enrolled thirty-nine men who were obliged to colonise 71,000 acres. This enrolment took place on 25 July; now thirty-six more Scots undertook to colonise 49,000 acres. It was unlikely that those enrolled in Edinburgh on 25 July would have come to Hay's attention. If they had reached Hay he would have granted far more than 75,000 acres as the total area requested by the Scots. It is likely that Hay knew about the requests of Lennox and Aubigny; he added 2,000 acres for each of them to the total lands he had received from Scotland.

The Scots wanted to colonise the whole of Ulster and the Council enrolled those who wanted to become undertakers. Hay now wrote to Salisbury on 6 August that he had received word from Scotland that there were many Scots wanting to settle upon Gaelic lands. The Scottish Council now undertook to send many planters to Ulster. Those who had applied for 2,000 acres would be granted small proportions. Hay said that it would be *a good means for peopling of these bounds*. The Scottish Council kept its word and enrolled many planters. At length the total land settled was 72,000 acres. Between 4 August and 14 September the Council accepted seven more men. A second total of thirty-nine potential undertakers made up the eventual figure of 75,000 acres. In all only sixteen of the seventy-eight planters were incorporated into the scheme. There were alterations in the colonisers' plans. Chief undertakers were appointed to preside over the lands. A new system was invented to choose the Scottish participants.

Candidates for colonisation came from many places, for example from Ayr, Dumbarton, Glasgow, Lanark, Wigtown, Edinburgh, Kinross, Perth, Dumfries, Stirling and Aberdeen. There was a large concentration of Edinburgh men out of two classifications that proposed colonisation in Ulster. There was a reduction in planting coming from the poorer south-western counties. In all groups small lairds or gentry constituted most of the applicants. There were no members of the aristocracy in either list and only one knight — Sir George Livingston was included in the second list. The rest of the planters came from either sons or younger brothers of gentry. There was a large number of townsmen, relatively speaking: between twenty-eight and eighteen per cent. The townsmen were normally burgesses. The Church was represented by the geographer, Mr Timothy Pont, a minister of Dumet, Caithness. Cautioners saw that the bonds for the lands were posted. Other tenants stood surety for one another. In some cases a tenant could become cautioner to several applicants. George Murray of Broughton provides an example of this. He applied for two thousand acres, and obtained Alexander Dunbar of Egirnes as his cautioner. In turn he became cautioner for Dunbar who also wanted two thousand acres. Murray became cautioner for three other men, all of them his neighbours in the south-west. Lord Ochiltree, although he did not apply for any land himself in 1609, became cautioner for his uncle, who owned land in Perthshire, together with three other men. Usually cautioners were the relatives of the principals, or, in the case of town dwellings, business associates.

Sixteen other men applied in 1609, eventually having land in Ulster; three men who did not apply acted as cautioners in 1609 and eventually became undertakers. The main significance of 1609 is that the Scots showed great enthusiasm for the colonisation of Ulster. Far more Scots applied than could be given land. It was the middle classes and not the aristocracy that showed this great interest in the province. Those that did apply perhaps did not realise the extent of the investment that they might have to make. The Scottish Council received official word of the alterations in the colonisation plans only in August 1609. From this date the Scottish Council would have nothing to do with the plantation plans. Ulster was divided into precincts, and the task of selecting the chief undertakers resided with King James. The undertakers were to make up the names which should settle under them in the different precincts. However, the Council was not excluded from subsequent plantation activity.

James delegated a committee of Scots who would normally live at court. This committee included such men as Alexander Hay, the Duke of Lennox and the Earl of Dunbar. A final list of undertakers was drawn up in the name of the Council. Chief undertakers had to be appointed by 19 March 1610. Sir John Davies noted that James was as yet not naming the undertakers. By 12 April the Earl of Abercorn knew that he was chosen. The first complete list of undertakers for a Scottish precinct had reached Dublin Castle by 19 April. Within the space of one month the chief undertakers for the precinct had been chosen, the ordinary undertakers selected, and their names forwarded to the committee of the Scottish Council, which in turn had set out from Dublin. It took a long time to communicate in the 17th century, so that James had probably made appointments of chief undertakers in early March or even in February.

Chichester advised that men of rank and quality should be included in the scheme, and others thought on similar lines. All those selected were either nobles or knights. There was a fairly even distribution between undertakers from the eastern and western parts of Scotland. There was perhaps a slight bias in favour of men from the west, because they were close to Ulster. However, a man's connections or his past career had as much to do with his inclusion as his geographical origin.

The Duke of Lennox and Lord Aubigny had been amongst the first Scots to show interest in Ulster. Lennox of course was a member of the Ulster plantation committee in England, but had also taken part in the plantation of Lewis in 1598. Lords Ochiltree and Bewly and the Earl of Abercorn had served the Crown loyally in the past. All were members of the Scottish Council and were made justices of the peace in one or more of the counties when that office was created in Scotland. Ochiltree was acting as a cautioner for those who had applied for Ulster land in 1609. He had great faith in the plantation scheme. The year before, he had led a successful expedition to the Isles to crush resistance to King James. This last service to the Crown made him amply suited to be appointed as an undertaker. Abercorn had served as one of the Scots commissioners for Scotland when the union with England made that a possibility. The nobles became chief undertakers at the request of King James. Ochiltree was recommended to the lord deputy later in the year. In Abercorn's case there was no reason why the king could not recommend him to be a cautioner. It was, however, difficult to get men to participate in the Ulster plantation plans. Many refused land when it was offered to them. Little else is known about the other men who became involved. Sir James Douglas of Spott, who was the bastard son of Regent Martin, and Sir James Howe of North Berwick were both loyal servants of James. They too may have been asked to serve the king. They may have been related to the Earl of Dunbar, and, as a member of the Scots plantation scheme, he would have been in a position to secure Ulster estates for them.

Dunbar had a voice in who should be appointed as undertakers, as in the case of Sir Alexander Hamilton. Hamilton had taken as his second wife Alison Howe, the earl's sister, but she died shortly after the marriage. Her husband maintained his friendship with his former brother-in-law. After Dunbar's death in 1612 it was common knowledge that Sir Alexander had become responsible for some of the earl's debts. There does not seem to be any reason why he was appointed as a chief undertaker. According to the privy council records he was involved in a number of disputes. He attained to the position of justice of the peace of Haddingtonshire in 1610, but this advancement must have been due to his connection with Dunbar, to whom, along with the chancellor, James had left the selection of these officials.

Sir Robert McClelland of Bombay was another official to be counted, but why he was chosen remains a mystery. In 1632 he was forty years of age or thereabouts. This meant that he was only fourteen when he became provost of Kirkcudbright in 1606 and eighteen when he obtained the command of the settlement of over 10,000 acres of Irish lands. His father had been a gentleman of the bedchamber, but he died in 1597, too early to help his son gain a distinguished position in Ulster. It is possible that Sir Robert McClelland obtained the preferment by way of Dunbar. The earl had supported the border commission and the young McClelland, in either 1609 or 1610, may have been made a member of the commission. However, Sir Robert is remembered because on occasion he could become violent, even by 17th-century standards. Another explanation for his preferment was James and his Council hoped to placate him or occupy him by sending him to Ulster. Now the process of selecting the ordinary undertakers took place. The final list was comprised of fifty men, the maximum assigned to any one precinct being eight and the minimum three. The appointments were made quite quickly. Their names were forwarded to Dublin by 15 May, and the Scottish desire to obtain Irish land had not been diminished since the previous year. Lord Balfour of Burley had declared that he had to reject a number of unsuitable applicants. However, it was not through the undertakers that men usually received their proportions. There was the possibility of court influence. Abercorn wrote to James on 12 April, concerned with the matter of preferment. He told James that he was making other appointments as well as to the lands in the region of Strabane in the north of Ireland. He told James that he was ready to plant twice this area. His efforts had met with no success, for the first three men to be granted lands had no connection with Abercorn. A long time passed until all the planters were added to the list to colonise Strabane.

James liked to interfere in the running of the plantation, for he exercised favouritism. Sir John Cunningham of Glengarnock and his uncle, also called James Cunningham, both obtained land in Lennox's precinct. Two years after the setting up of the plantation James wrote to the lord deputy on their behalf saying that the appointments were made on the merits of the undertakers concerned. There were also several other colonisers known to the king. Ten of the fifty being royal servants, at least three others had royal connections, and another three held important positions in Scotland. They would have had easy access to important officials. Many entered the scheme at James's request, and approximately one third of the ordinary Scots undertakers were able to petition the Crown or to be enlisted by the king.

Responsibility for the selection of the ordinary undertakers lay theoretically in the hands of the principal men. There were close family ties as patronage was dispensed with. There was the chief undertaker, but there were also appointments made outside the ordinary system. John and Cuthbert Cunningham obtained proportions through the influence of Sir James Cunningham of Glengarnock. Thirty-one of the appointments were made, or sixty per cent of the total. Among the remaining forty per cent there was often a geographical link if not one of blood. Some undertakers were government servants, related to their chief undertaker as far as can be determined. Henry Acheson and William Lander both came from Edinburgh, and both obtained land in the precinct under the direction of Sir James Douglas. Many of these undertakers came from the east of Scotland. One of these, George Smailholm, was chosen instead of the other well-qualified applicants, but it is not known why.

There was a geographical bond between planters who existed in the extreme south-west. Some undertakers obtained land in Donegal in the precinct of Boylagh and Banagh. None were related to the chief undertaker, Sir Robert McClelland, even though he came from the same area. One of them, George Murray of Broughton, had influence at court, and he put up sureties for three other planters in 1609 when they had applied for land; and two others were related to Lord Garlies, a very influential person. The chief undertaker of the Donegal plantation was only eighteen years of age. It is possible that Murray and William Stewart of Mains, brother of Lord Garlies, acted jointly in choosing planters for Irish land. Murray and Stewart received middle-sized proportions, whilst the other undertakers were given only small amounts of land. Murray and Stewart's names headed the list of ordinary undertakers.

There are eight other men whose role in the plantation has not been explained. The Earl of Abercorn became the chief undertaker in Strabane, but the list sent to Dublin Castle did not include his name. The list named only three men, none of whom had any connection with the earl. Another fifty-nine men received lands in those areas specifically set aside for the Scottish plantation. In all three were sixty-one Scots who were initially granted lands in the escheated areas. A look at the general distribution of land in Scottish areas is useful. There were about three areas of concentration. First there was the north-west of the Lowlands, including Ayrshire, Renfrewshire, north Lanarkshire and Dumbartonshire. Still in the west of the Wigtownshire-Kirkcudbrightshire district, most of the colonisers were confined to the Whithorn peninsula. In the east there was the Edinburgh-Haddingshire area. There was also a small concentration in Ayrshire. These areas were generally represented by a few men, for example south of Aberdeen and down to the Firth of Forth. The lairds from the wild borders areas were not represented; a single man from Berwickshire being the only exception.

The west of Scotland contributed more to the plantation situation, but this bias towards the west was slight; there was a less equal division between the west and the east. This seemed to indicate an attempt at partial division of Irish spoils. Westerners were encouraged to participate in the place of the easterners. There was a preponderance of easterners. The government tried to increase the number of planters for the west, presumably because it was thought that the planters from the west would have less difficulty in transporting tenants and provisions to Ulster.

Some of the colonisers were men of high social standing. Noblemen became chief undertakers, and there were eleven knights amongst the ordinary planters, as opposed to only one coloniser who had applied in 1608. As a result of the policies of introducing quality people there was a reduction in the number of farmers involved. Three townsmen who became involved in the plantation for the first time in 1610 were all royal servants. The middle classes were to be excluded in favour of the lords. The gentry found it easier than the townsmen to obtain tenants. The lairds were used to managing estates, but there were the towns as well as the countryside. This might have meant that the townsmen had a wrong attitude towards the plantation. Merchants and burgesses looked at the plantation in purely economic terms, but Chichester remarked that the planters would reap more honour than profit in the scheme. There were to be no instant rewards. The gentry were the traditional middle classes and they could effectively contain any rebellion of the Ulster Gaels. The question was whether the resources of the undertakers were adequate to meet the demands made on them.

The income of a group of men in the 17th century is hard to estimate. Estimates of Scots incomes are vulnerable because of the few records of the state of affairs that have remained. It is the task of the historian to determine the extent of their income on the eve of their setting out for Ulster. The average yearly income of the Scots lairds was between £1,700 and £1,800 (Scots) — or approximately £150 sterling. This figure can be used in assessing the income of the various planters. Turning first to the chief undertakers, it is certain that the two main undertakers, the Duke of Lennox and Lord Aubigny, had incomes in excess of these figures. They were relations of King James and were in constant attendance at court, and they were in a position to receive gifts. In 1608 James gave Lord Aubigny £1,000 sterling per annum. Lord Abercorn was also wealthy. Upon his death in 1618 his estate was calculated at £23,255 10s 0d (Scots). He had great debts, which reduced the value of his legacy, but he still remained as one of Scotland's landowners.

Two other noblemen were amongst the Scots undertakers, but they were less well off. Lord Burley left an estate of only £703 4s 6d (Scots) — just under £60 sterling — when he died in 1619. There were also those of Lord Ochiltree, whose affairs were in an even worse condition. By 1613 he had to sell both his title and his Scottish estates to his cousin, Sir James Stewart of Killeith, which left him only with land he owned in Ulster. He had led an expedition to subjugate the Isles in 1608, which was largely responsible for his serious financial state. From 1610 onwards he borrowed heavily, and the only way of developing his plantation was by raising loans.

Much less is known about the financial position of the remaining three undertakers. Sir John Howe of Berwick and Sir James Douglas of Spott were royal servants, so their income perhaps was above average. Douglas received many gifts from King James. We know even less about Sir Alexander Hamilton of Innerwick — he had acted for the Earl of Dunbar's debts, which implies that he was not poor. There was Sir Robert McClelland of Bombay, who was in debt at the very start of the plantation. However, he did not become seriously involved in Ulster affairs until 1617 and 1618. He had leased land belonging to two of the London Companies in Londonderry. He was able to raise large sums of money without difficulty. By 1625, however, his financial position had become perilous and this was partly due to the rent he owed to the London Companies. The rent was high; he was also responsible for raising a company of troops for King Charles I. It may be he concluded from this that the land's income was above average.

Much less material is extant about the activities of the ordinary undertakers. It is necessary to place them in categories rather than to give a man-to-man analysis. Only three testaments about the activities of the ordinary planters have survived. Of these the most important is the information regarding Sir Claud Hamilton of Schawfield. He purchased land of James Haig's proportion in 1612. Beyond this he invested little in Ulster before his death in 1615. He had been collecting rent from Irish tenants on his own proportion before his death. He obtained returns from his Irish investment. He died in the middle of October. His estate recorded the crops that were ready for harvesting. The estimate of the crops either reaped or still standing in the fields was £2,413 6s 8d (Scots). There are no records of labour costs. From other lands the estimated yield was £1,180 9s 6d (Scots). He was owed money from some of his tenants and for tithes, which amounted to £1,007 9s 0d (Scots). This gave him a generous income of £3,751 12s 9d (Scots), to which must be added the return from other stock. He may have received gifts not recorded in these statements. The figures do not take into account property owned by his wife. His Scottish lands brought in an income of between £200 and £300 sterling per year — considerably more than the Scots gentry. Sir Claud was therefore amongst the richer undertakers, being a knight, a royal servant and the brother of an earl. About half the ordinary Scots undertakers were of the same social class as Claud, and they had incomes above average for the Scottish gentry, even though not as high as Claud himself. This group would include the royal servants, all the knights, the relatives of noblemen and such men as Thomas Moneypenny of Kilkeel and Claud Hamilton of Creichness, whom the Scots Council described as a gentleman of worth.

Many lairds had large amounts of money and property. Bernard Linsay, dying in 1626, left a free estate. He was amongst the numerous Scots to receive a gift from the Crown in 1608, and another gift was given to him in 1610 just before the start of the plantation. James Gibb received a pension of £200 sterling per annum in 1614. The Scots Guard was reduced in 1611 and its commander, Sir Robert Hepburn, was granted a yearly pension of

£100 sterling, which was only a supplement to his income from his estates and a coal mine. Sir Robert Wishart of Pittarro and Sir James Cunningham of Glengarnock were exceptions to the rule, and Wishart was described by an enemy in Ireland as having begged for land in the country. Yet he may not have been entirely impoverished, for he was made one of the justices of the peace for Kincardineshire in 1610; and in 1611 he put up 3,000 marks for a friend. When Sir James Cunningham of Glengarnock died in 1623 he left his widow destitute, so that in 1627 King Charles I had to intervene on her behalf. However, prior to the plantation he was a man of considerable means. He had a castle in Ayrshire, and it was described as being a considerable place. He had lands in four other counties apart from Ayrshire, but by 1610 he was on the verge of bankruptcy. The other colonisers had only small incomes; a lot below average. When Sir John Ralstom's father died in 1623 he left only £371 10s 0d (Scots) in free estate — or nearly £30 sterling. Of this the undertakers received only £30. There were many exceptions, and William Stewart Dundaff borrowed 4,000 marks in 1610, yet he has been included in the impoverished group.

The true state of monetary affairs concerning the Scots colonisers comes from England. When some Englishmen applied for land in Ulster, they wanted to know how much the Scots planters were worth. Thirteen Englishmen received proportions, or just under a quarter of the Englishmen that had applied. They had exaggerated their own wealth in order to be accepted. Four declared incomes below £150 sterling per year, the lowest being £84. Seven ranged between £159 and £300, and of the two remaining, one had an income of £400 per annum, and another claimed an estate worth £1,500. The majority had incomes exceeding those of the Scots colonisers. There were of course poorer English undertakers. Seventy per cent of the English undertakers received grants of 1,500 acres or more; just under fifty per cent of a sample received proportions of this size. The income of the richer Scots was approximately equal to those of the poorer Englishmen. This was in keeping with the fact that England was a richer country than Scotland. It was stated that the Scots arrived with great enthusiasm despite their inferior financial position. The English and Scots had now the task of transforming the Ulster plantation lands into profitable units. Motivation for profit and ambition were obviously part of the early 17th-century Ulster scene, but it should be mentioned that some of the Scots became colonisers after a personal request from King James.

Chapter Six

The Plantation Goes Under Way

By 15 May 1610 most of the important planters had been appointed and their money forwarded to London. Agents were supposed to be in Ireland by 24 June. However, conditions had to be settled before the colonisers or planters took up their lots, which could not be settled in a month or two. Thus from the beginning the planters were working behind the schedule that had been established. Patents had to be issued for the lands concerned, a process that was only begun at the end of April 1610 when a commission was formed in England to draw up the relevant documents. In the case of the Scots there was a further delay. They had been born prior to King James's accession to the English throne, so they remained technically foreigners and could not enjoy full property rights in either England or Ireland. An act passed in Mary's reign forbade the Scots from legally entering the country. King James, however, directed that all patents passed to the Scots should contain a clause making them both denizens of England and Ireland, thus securing their rights to the lands. But permission to carry this out was sent to the English chancellor only by 11 May 1610. A little while before this James must have sent orders to his northern privy council to help in the distribution of patents. On 22 May the Council issued a proclamation requiring undertakers to appear before the Council upon the following Tuesday so that the conditions of the Ulster plantation should be secure.

However, it was not practical that large numbers of planters should make their journeys to Ulster and to Dublin straight away. Only in three cases have the dates of bonds survived, the earliest dated 20 July and the other two 3 July and 28 August. Lord Burley was provided for after he obtained his patent, dated 29 June. In most cases the deadline had passed before the coming of the colonisers. Most of the others received their patents later. The majority were passed either in July or August, although three were still being issued as legal title to land as late as 1612 and 1613. Another cause of delay was the obtaining of suitable men to become colonisers. The planters were busy trying to obtain men of wealth to take up the leases on Ulster lands and thus reduce costs. In this they were met with the same problem that beset King James when they first tried to settle in the north of Ireland. Those of adequate means were not willing to risk their fortunes on a venture so fraught with risks as the colonisation of Ulster. To engage those without funds or money would only end in disaster. Now Lord Aubigny, the courtier cousin of the king, had as early as May begun negotiations to pass all his colonisation responsibilities to Hamilton. As a result of this Aubigny sold his proportions to Sir James. As a result of Hamilton's report, although written about the English position, light is thrown upon what was happening in Scotland. Many sought companions to accompany them, but some must have gradually realised how much money they would have to invest in Ulster.

On 9 June King James issued final orders for the formation of a commission, headed by the lord deputy, to oversee the establishment of the undertakers on their proportions. Chichester delayed the departure for Ulster in order to obtain sufficient supplies to support the army, which he would use to confiscate lands from the natives so that the Ulster plantation could be set up. By 4 August Chichester and his commissioners had reached Cavan, part of nine-county Ulster, where he began the process of colonisation. They impressed the Irish with their army. Undertakers had to appear before the commission with warrants of possession to their respective proportions. An oath of supremacy had to be taken, granting licenses for the settlement of areas. Areas of wood and bog were assigned to each proportion.

The next stop for the colonisers was Devenish in County Fermanagh. Calderwood said that his countrymen began to depart for Ulster in July, but the beginning of August seems a more likely date. Lord Burley was one of the first Scots to arrive in Ireland. He received a letter of recommendation from the Scots Council, addressed to the lord deputy, Chichester, and dated 2 August. Bernard Lindsey, a groom of the bedchamber, received letters of recommendation the next day. The little band of colonisers made their way west. Upon reaching Ayr, the middle classes entertained them with *sweetmeats and sugar*. Now they were ready to sail to Ulster, and they were able to join Chichester's party in Fermanagh by 13 August. Warrants of possession were issued. The commissions passed from county to county in Ulster, and the majority of Scots were assured of possession of their proportions.

About forty-five men appeared personally or sent agents to represent them. Bernard Lindsey joined the commissioners in Fermanagh and occupied them on a circuit of Ulster until they reached County Tyrone where he held land. There were others, who arrived after the commissioners had left the vicinity, and they informed the deputy and his companions. They took out warrants for possession, and presumably hurried off to view their new estates. The Scots passed through Ulster during the late summer and early autumn of 1610, and they had mixed feelings about the territory they were given to settle. There is some evidence to suggest that the famines and ravages wrought by war were going away. Cavan was relatively well populated and was never the scene of much fighting. Cavan was well populated by 1608, and there were the confiscated O'Neill lands which were growing rich. County Fermanagh had natural beauty, and the poet, Sir John Davies, also a lawyer, sung the praises of the plantation scheme. Lord Burley, whose land lay in County Cavan, upon returning home from Scotland made a favourable report about Ulster to Sir Alexander Hay. Ulster, despite its natural beauty, was a ravaged land. One report stated that there was only one church with a roof intact. George Smailholm, a resident of Leith, took one look at his proportion of land and returned home, refusing to have anything more to do with the plantation.

The Scots had received land in County Donegal and the same reaction as in Cavan must have transpired even though they did not rent with the same promptitude. These lands were occupied in the extreme western part of the province abutting the sea on a peninsula that jutted out into the Atlantic Ocean. Donegal was full of challenges, more challenges than in the other Ulster counties. The plantations were exposed to storms that swept in from the west. The Donegal mountains shut the county off from the rest of Ulster. The group of Wigtownshiremen who undertook to settle the area would have to raise crops in spite of the Atlantic winds. The second plantation in Donegal met with a more favourable outcome. Portlough, which occupied the northern part of the barony of Raphoe, lay between the River Foyle and Lough Swilly, and was bounded in the north by the barony of Inishowen. In the parish maps of the 17th century the area is said to have had good soils.

Looking out across the River Foyle from Portlough, lay the Earl of Abercorn's precinct — the barony of Strabane in County Tyrone. It contained much mountainous land. There were also stretches of some good arable land, particularly along the east bank of the River Foyle where much of Abercorn's land was situated; but there was bog bordering the river. The second Scottish precinct in Tyrone, overseen by Mountjoy, consisted of the northern section of the barony of Dungannon. It lay along the western shores of Lough Neagh and the land was reasonably fertile.

In Armagh the Scots received the northern part of the barony of the Fews, but the southern section lay in the hands of the Gaels and the Church. However, the Fews had a lot of mountainous infertile land, but the section that the Scots received was fertile. To the south, in the parish of Cregan, bogs abounded, while in the north of the parish, despite bogs and mountains, grazing and cultivation took place. In all the precincts the chief undertakers received the best land. Ochiltree's lands bordered Lough Neagh. Both of Abercorn's lay along the River Foyle, and Lennox's stood on the opposite bank. In County Fermanagh, Lord Burley's land faced upper Lough Erne, consisting of land on either side of the lough. The chief undertaker in Magheraboy possessed the largest shoreline along lower Lough Erne. There were three remaining precincts; the lands set aside for colonisation seemed to be less obvious than elsewhere, but in Cavan they were located next to the escheated counties. The exposed lands in Boylagh and Banagh enjoyed most protection from the sea, and were granted to Sir Robert McClelland. From the very start of the plantation those who were first to receive land found it easiest to develop.

Many of the Scots who had put their names forward for the colonisation of Ulster in 1610 often brought friends and business associates with them. Lord Deputy Chichester remarked that the Scots arrived with more planters than the English. Calderwood noted that the gentry went first to look at their estates; many tenants accompanied them. The Scottish Secretary of State was even more emphatic. He wrote that the west-country people of the common sort flocked over to Ireland in so great numbers, but much of the land lay waste for want of tenants. However, there does not seem to have been an immediate influx of settlers into Ulster. Even after one year the number of Scots in Ulster amounted to only a few hundred. Those tenants eagerly seized the opportunities available in rural Ulster, and initially planters had no trouble in getting men to join them.

Now in Ulster the undertakers set the colonisers to work. Buildings had to be erected and the land had to be ploughed and sown. The Scots had brought numerous men with them but they were confronted with a problem not faced by their less enthusiastic English colleagues. There were delays in getting the plantation under way, and this meant that the season had advanced too far for the colonisers to harvest crops that year. Winter supplies were imported at great cost or obtained from the local population. The Scots were the first to negotiate with the Irish, promising to intervene on their behalf with King James, if in return they would supply money or provisions. The planters received indirect support from the plantation commission. The British were in danger of starving to death. A proclamation was issued in August permitting the Gaels to remain on their lands until the following May or on condition that they paid rent to the undertakers.

The plantation started to run into difficulties. The Scots laid aside any ambitions to become rich overnight by planting Ulster's soil. It would be difficult to transform natural beauty into hard cash. Smailholm was not the only Scot to visit Ulster in 1610, never to return. These Scots must have let Chichester know of the demoralised state they were in. The lord deputy was aware that the entire plantation of Ulster might come about in his lifetime. Only determined planters with capital to see themselves through a bad patch were eligible to colonise Ulster, and they had to forget about a quick profit. They might be able to make the scheme a success. However, Chichester did not despair. Some undertakers sought immediate rewards;

some left Ulster when they realised that there was not a chance of a substantial profit, but these were a minority. Most of the Scots persevered over a two- or three-year period.

In the New Year of 1610 it was essential to insure that the proposed scheme for the Ulster plantation went under way. The undertakers were inclined to evade the conditions in relation to the land. The policy was that only British settlers should plant with British tenants alone. It was ordered that all colonisers should be present in Ulster by 1 May 1611. A proclamation to this effect was published on 13 April. It included measures for the forfeiture of patents and bonds as well as a punishment for those who did not cooperate. The undertakers were busy. During the winter months they sent men to settle on the land. Sir John Davies reported that Dublin was full of planters ready to make their way north to Ulster. There were Englishmen, but the Scots were also using the Ulster ports. One coloniser, who had leased land from an undertaker, had made seven voyages to Ulster by April 1611.

By May some of the Scots undertakers had been referred to the lord deputy either to settle issues which they felt might jeopardise the success of the plantation or to obtain special privileges. Lord Burley was assured that he would not come under attack from the Irish chiefs from which he obtained land. The Earl of Abercorn was able to draw twenty-five men from the Irish army to assist him in planting the land and in erecting colonial-style buildings. Other colonisers appealed to King James in land disputes, and one coloniser received a recommendation for special help as a result of the favourable impression he had made with Chichester, the lord deputy. Abercorn's land lay in a particularly hostile area. Those who did not reach Ireland by 1 May were threatened with further confiscation of land. The lord deputy remembered that the planters were slow in arriving. The English privy council dealt with matters pertaining to Ulster. The undertakers were accused of having been slack. Those present on their proportions had done little more than to collect lime and sometimes a little stone for help in building. However, it was the British government's intent to keep as many Irishmen on the land as possible, for they alone could supply transport to the more remote proportions. Usually they provided the only source of labour for growing food. If the Ulster plantation was to survive, then something had to be done immediately. As a result London sent Sir George Carew to inquire into the various aspects of Irish administration. The British government was concerned about the progress, or lack of it, in the Ulster plantation and the colonisation of the north.

Carew had arrived in Dublin about three weeks later, and he had adequate qualifications for his task. He knew the country well, having spent twelve years in Ireland between 1574 and 1603, either as a soldier or an official of the Irish government. In his final years in Ireland he rose to the post of President of Munster. He was to undertake with others a survey of Ulster.

He made an estimate of the Scots migration in Ulster during the first years. It is essential to assess the degree of the survey's accuracy, so that it is useful to examine the procedure of the surveyors before any analysis can be made of the findings. Carew and his fellow commissioners, including the lord deputy, left Dublin at the end of July. They travelled through some of the counties that would not be affected by the colonisation process. They followed a route that took them from Dundalk to Newry, then on to Carrickfergus and Dunluce Castle. They arrived at Londonderry on 14 August. From Londonderry they went on a tour of Ulster. They went to Donegal first, then south to Enniskillen, which they had reached by the 25th. Turning north again it took them five days to pass through County Tyrone to Dungannon. In Dungannon they again turned south to arrive at Armagh two days later. From Armagh they returned to Dublin, reaching it on 5 September. The expedition had taken place in great haste, for Carew was left out. They viewed in person the work of some of the planters, and they derived most of their information from governors or sheriffs of the particular counties. Carew was pleased with the help the planters had given. However, the population estimates came from a variety of sources, but he expressed a view that had the numbers been large the information given would almost have been meaningless. There were few takers for the Ulster plantation and in estimates the margin of error could be as much as fifty per cent. A rough guide is possible to the state of the Ulster plantation from Carew's report.

At the time of Carew's survey fifty-nine undertakers are recorded. Only forty-two were agents to look after the land. Five more had sent servants, although no agent was present. There was the question of the colonisers' buildings. A mandate had been sent by 1 November 1611 that all houses required for tenants were to be constructed. Only twenty-five men had made a start in any permanent building. Despite the previously dry winter, work on the land had been started on only six proportions, although the presence of horses and mares, as in the case of oxen, shows that at least fourteen more proportions were available for cultivation by the time the commissioners completed their circuit.

Stock was scarce in Ulster and the planters brought most of their livestock over from Scotland. The Carew survey said that animals were *brought over* or *sent*. In one instance the commissioners reported that a Scot had brought over some barons and horses and were buying cattle on a daily basis. The planter was sometimes able to supplement imports with local purchases. Population figures are unreliable. Several of the lands had some tenants. In other cases it was not easy to make a population assessment, for the numbers may have referred to families, adults or men. There is also the question of the number of Scottish women present. In 1622 thirty-nine families were recorded as being on English land; thirteen families contained more men that women, whereas only in eight families did the women outnumber the men. The average ratio of men to women was sixty-eight to thirty-nine; the average ratio for women being slightly less. A Scots immigrant family was little different from its English counterpart. There must have been at least one and a half Scottish women present for every Scottish male. By Carew's calculation 350 adults, including women, settled on the estates.

The nationality of the undertakers does not seem to be important. In regard to the lands held by Abercorn and Sir George Hamilton, not all came from Scotland. It was pointed out that the inhabitants of the Scottish estates came from both England and Scotland; otherwise the other land workers were regarded as British. It was reasonable to assume that all the lands allotted to Scotsmen came from Scotland. They had not snapped up the land beyond their own proportions, except in the towns of Lifford and Donegal where they had a strong presence.

The Scottish immigrants can be divided into three categories. First of all there was the freeholder, described as gentry, who were probably relations of the undertakers. Secondly there were the leaseholders and cottagers, who must have been of a common sort, described as flocking into Ulster by the Scottish Secretary. Thirdly there were the artisans, such as masons, who helped with the building operations, and servants who looked after the undertakers' personal effects and livestock. Ministers of religion followed in the footsteps of the colonisers. In many cases wives and their families accompanied their husbands, but it is certain that men outnumbered women. One Michael Balfour was reported to have brought over to Ulster four women servants, who appear to have been unmarried, but this is the only reference to women associated with a family. The extent of the plantation differed greatly from county to county and indeed from proportion to proportion. Two precincts, the Fews in Armagh and Mountjoy in Tyrone were better managed than the other plantations. Strabane and Knockninny did not fall far behind. In Donegal, Portlough was better settled than the Boylagh and Banagh. Here, so far, undertakers were present so that they could appoint an *Agnes gennall* to supervise the other agents. In Cavan, in only one of the proportions, there was not anything significantly accomplished. Here a majority of colonisers were present.

If a precinct was highly accessible the coloniser experienced great success. The exception to this rule was Fermanagh where Magheraboy was more easily approached than Knockninny, but less well developed. If we examine the basics elsewhere, we find again that accessibility was of prime importance. The planter had to be able to finance his operation and upon this hinged the success or failure of the project. We have seen that the undertakers obtained the most fertile regions, while the second best went to the relatives of the principal men or to King James's favourites. Cost depended to some extent directly upon accessibility. If land proportions were not remote, the colonisers had greater success. A man of modest means on a favourite piece of land might prosper while a rich companion whose lands lay far off from the roots might fail in his endeavours. In the Fews, in Armagh, four out of the five planters had begun building. The agent of the fifth, the chief undertaker, arrived with fifteen undertenants after the commissioners had left the country. Four of these men belonged to a group of planters, who were above average in wealth. They enjoyed the added advantage of being fairly close to Scotland and next to County Down, the most English county in Ulster. They were able to make remarkable progress. Sir Claud Hamilton of Creichness had planted five families, making up sixteen persons. He had eighty cows and fourteen horses on his land, and was now in the process of eventually building a planter's bawn, or fortified manor house, like the planter's castle at Ballygally on the Antrim coast. Sir James Craig had also sown and reaped oats and barley. He settled four British families and had begun to build a mill. The report of the commissioners on other men in the precinct recorded a move of property in the colonised lands.

At Mountjoy, Lord Ochiltree and Sir Robert Hepburn had greatly achieved. Both had land in the east of the precinct and there was easy access to their lands by water. Sir Robert Hepburn was amongst the most wealthy of the undertakers. However, Ochiltree had to sell his Scottish estates, but he had enough funds left to undertake the Ulster colonisation. He arrived in Ulster after the commissioners had left Tyrone. When he arrived he had brought with him thirty-three undertenants. By the time the undertakers reached the lands thirteen houses stood within the ruins of an old fort, about which the bawn was to be situated. Plans for the construction of a stone castle were also in progress. The commissioners found two ploughs at work on the land and fifty cows already there with heifers on the way. These heifers had been landed at Island Magee, which points to the fact that the safest route was overland through Antrim, rather than south through Coleraine, which had been made safe by Chichester's efforts before 1610.

Hepburn's lot had progressed more than Ochiltree's. Sir Robert enjoyed a good harvest and reaped sixteen horse lands of corn during 1611. He was resident in person with seven families settled on the land, which made up twenty-nine persons in all and he kept a total of 140 cows. The construction of a stone house had begun and materials for more buildings were being gathered. There was prosperous land inland, but not as advanced as Ochiltree's and Hepburn's. The most backward of them was George Crawford's of Lefnoreis. He had arrived as an Irish agent and he started gathering materials for building, but no Scots were settled, nor would they be in the future. In July 1610, just before the plantation had begun, Crawford was lodged in Edinburgh, and in 1609 his son and heir, also called George, had been lodged in Blackness Castle for feuding. Sixteen were fined 10,000 marks while Carew was informed that their father was dead. There was not much money available to Crawford to set up an Irish estate.

A similar pattern prevailed at Strabane. The two most illustrious undertakers, the Earl of Abercorn and his brother, Sir George Hamilton, had lands bordering on the River Foyle. Near Strabane, Abercorn and his followers built four large thatched timber houses with foundations of oak. Around these arose a wall 116 feet long by eighty-seven feet wide. Before May 1611 his tenants had built thirty-two houses with inclined rafters, and since that date another twenty-eight houses. Each house contained one family, each consisting of three persons. Sixty families and one hundred and eighty adults resided on Abercorn's lands. The earl may have obtained tenants from the Scots already in Ulster since the reign of Queen Elizabeth I. However, they had their homes burned down by O'Doherty in 1608. Other tenants may have come from the company of Scots soldiers stationed in Ulster under Captain William Stewart. In the spring Abercorn was permitted to order twenty-five men from the Irish Army to help with the colonisation progress. Materials had been gathered for the construction the following year of a castle and bawns. There was also a brewery and one hundred and twenty cattle, which indicates that the plantation was becoming self-sufficient. Abercorn's brother, Sir George, had also made great progress, but not of such a spectacular nature. Sir Thomas Boyd had easy access to his land, and he was resident with his family and started to gather building materials. In the hinterland of the barony, the two men tried to farm the mountainous regions. The other three had tried to assert themselves, but settlement never exceeded one family.

Comparative wealth and good locations were the backbone of the plantation of Ulster. Three out of the four men at Knockninny possessed estates lying along the shores of upper Lough Erne. Thomas Moneypenny, whose lands lay inland, was described by the Scottish Council as a good trustworthy gentleman. He had been involved in the Lewis venture, so he possessed expertise in colonisation. Twenty-four adults were living on his lands and seventy had been shipped over from Scotland. Provisions for the following winter had been assured for there was a very good harvest. A house containing fourteen rooms had been completed. In County Cavan, Sir Alexander Hamilton's achievements were above those of his competitors. In Donegal — in Boylagh and Banagh — the men had tried to establish a position for they were distant relations of King James. George Murray was a former gentleman of the bedchamber.

Financial resources of the average coloniser and geographical location were important in the success of the project, but energy and personal ambition for aggrandisement were also required. Let us look at Portlough as an example: the chief undertaker here was the Duke of Lennox, and he was probably the richest of the Scots colonisers. His lands lay along the banks of the River Foyle, facing Abercorn's lands. His lands were the most backward in relation to the other sites in the Ulster plantation. He was involved in court affairs, which led to the neglect of his Ulster duties. The same was true of James Gibb and William Fowler, both courtiers who performed badly at Magheraboy. On Lennox's lands the Cunninghams were leading lights, and James had encouraged them personally to make roots in Ulster. Six families were planted, as well as another six servants on the land, and all but one had started to build. Geographical location was a most important consideration, for they could all reach their land by sea via Lough Swilley, or, as in the case of James Cunningham, through Londonderry, which lay only six miles east of his lands. Captain William Stewart was a servitor and a Scot, and his building activities were well advanced, although as a servitor he was obliged not to introduce British tenants. There is no evidence that there was any Scots settlement on his lands at this time.

It is difficult to assess the entire cost of the Ulster plantation, and few records have survived, which seems to be unusual; and those that have survived are a bit sketchy. However, it is possible to reconstruct. A few planters had the run of their lands, upon which they could erect houses, but this was unusual. Land was usually in a virgin state to begin with. Carew's survey comprised and represented one year's work from the time the colonisers set up camp. The outlay in the initial year was probably higher than in the other years. There was a great necessity to bring over livestock. The new lands had been established and there was no need for a fresh influx of colonisers. Income from this time was probably small since the land was underdeveloped; the collection of rent from the Irish must have been difficult to start with. Financial troubles confronted the Scots and this illustrates the great burden on the undertakers' resources. The operation was divided into four lots: the construction of buildings, the cultivation of the land, the importing of tenants, and the provision of tenants once they had arrived. In 1625 Sir Robert McClelland said that he had spent £60 sterling building two mills and four malt kilns which he described as the cheapest kind in Ireland. McClelland also claimed that he had spent £300 sterling building six stone houses and a stone bawn. Three years before, an Englishman, who had fallen heir to the lands at Strabane said that he could build a stone house surrounded by a bawn sixteen feet high for £400 sterling. Also in 1625 Sir William Stewart, the former Scottish Secretary, said that to build a good strong castle with a wall three and a half feet thick, with five turrets, two courts, a gatehouse and a bawn surrounding it, along with another bawn within the existing bawn, cost £1,200 sterling. However, estimates of this kind of building were rare. It is probably true to state that the building of these bawns and castles must have cost at least £600 sterling.

The cost of establishing livestock on Ulster soil largely depended upon the wealth in terms of cattle that a planter possessed back in the home country of Scotland. If he was able to spare some animals for his Irish estate, the cost of obtaining Ulster land was that much less. The cost of a head of cattle at the beginning of the plantation was between £1 and £1 5s. These prices can be compared with cattle shipped directly from Scotland into Ulster. A commission was set up in 1616 to examine the possibility of setting up a ferry service between Scotland and Ulster at Donaghadee, County Down. It was recommended that one shilling and sixpence to two shillings per animal should be charged for shipping cattle according to the season. The passage between Scotland and Ulster was not the only threat the colony laboured under, and the price recommended by the commission may have been artificially low, but it was probably not more than five shillings a beast for a planter to remove his livestock from Scotland to Ulster's virgin land. In other words, a planter with a surplus of cattle in Scotland could stock his land for a quarter of what it cost to buy cattle in Ulster.

Some tenants made their own way to Ulster, whilst undertakers had to pay the passage of others. The introduction of eighty to one hundred persons into Ulster cost in the region of £200. It cost only about £55 sterling to transport the 200 Scots soldiers into the province in 1608. The cost covered food for the journey and other transport charges. In 1608 the Scots travelled from Ayr to Carrickfergus, whilst Sir Robert McClelland had probably to draw his people from Kirkcudbright to Coleraine. There was also the task of supporting a settlement before it became self-sufficient. By 1623 one planter had become self-sufficient, and he looked after his tenants. It is not clear how many undertakers took similar care of those under them. However, it was complained that the cost of land was high. One of the main problems was the supply of food for the colonisers. Even the most modest plantation cost over £500 sterling, and more elaborate operations could cost £1,500 sterling or more. If the custom was not carried out properly, this could mean heavy expenditure. By 1613 over £3,000 sterling had been spent on the Haberdashers' lands or proportions, either by the company itself or by Adrian Moore and William Freeman. In April 1611 the company transferred its interests to those two persons. Despite the intensive efforts at colonisation the plantation was regarded as most backward in 1615. Expenses on this scale would have ruined the most wealthy of the Scots.

Abercorn's plantation contained about one hundred British settlers in 1611, and many of those may have been in Ulster when he arrived. None of the Scots had erected large buildings. Wooden houses had been built and stone ones started. Numerous tenants had been imported, along with livestock. Winter provisions were also supplied. Claud Hamilton of Creichness held land in Armagh. He had brought with him sixteen men and women. They were worth £2 0s 5d per head, and passage and provisions for the colonisers must have been required at £20 to £30 sterling, or more if the tenants came from Haddingtonshire, Hamilton's own county. The land supported eighty cows and fourteen horses and, if they had been acquired from Hamilton's own Scottish estate, they would have cost between £20 and £25 to transport — if any were bought the outlay must have been much greater.

The commission found six masons building a bawn, presumably of wood. Three houses, also of wood, were being constructed. These buildings can hardly have cost less than Sir Robert McClelland's two inexpensive mills and four malt kilns. Hamilton's expenses for the first year amounted to over £100 sterling. However, this does not take into account such necessities as weapons, which by agreement he was obliged to supply to his tenants. Abercorn, Ochiltree and Burley spent more than Claud Hamilton. Many others spent less, and few planters enjoyed an income of over £200. There was great strain on the colonisers to farm the lands. Events in Scotland could affect the plantation. James Haig of Bemerside, Berwickshire, never set foot in Ireland because of problems at home. He became involved in disputes in Scotland over parts of his own lands. There was delay in starting the plantation, and all the planters were supposed to be in Ireland by 24 June. The loss of more time meant that the Scots could only begin work as the bad weather approached. Matters were put to rights quite rapidly and a large number of men had reached Ireland by the autumn of 1610. As Carew reported, only some planters had started to work a year after the deadline. The plantation was meant to go ahead two months after the conditions were published. If the British government had left Ulster alone until the spring of 1611, the planters would have had time to collect both men and money. They could have started the colonisation process with an entire summer ahead of them. The plantation — even in the most favourable lands — was a hazardous business, particularly for those of slender purse and for those in isolated spots. After the first year rents and crops went to support the beginning of the English colonisation, particularly in Ulster. Other problems also had started to surface, which were to have a serious effect on both rich and poor.

Chapter 7

The Plantation's Progress

Despite Carew's predictions about the plantation, things did not go according to plan. In 1612 the plantation was on its way. It was also stated that Ulster was not organised sufficiently to yield good profits from colonisation. King James had complained about the unenthusiastic attitudes of the colonisers, and James also received word of the stark proceedings in the Ulster plantation. Many of the planters were of mean ability and it was hard to form an impression of the plantation as a whole. King James's informants did little to enlighten the situation. James ordered Chichester to initiate a new survey on the entire state of the plantation. The king ordered Chichester not to fear the situation.

King James had appeared to become concerned about the Ulster situation, and the feeling of the other planters bordered on despair. One authority stated that the British undertakers would never import English or Scottish tenants while they could obtain lands from the Gaels. The number of immigrants of British families to Ulster was extremely high. Long-term leases were not popular, for the land was liable to provide higher rents when planted. The Gaels were willing to pay higher rents than their English and Scots competitors. Chichester had complained that the colonisers were making slow progress towards the completion of the plantation. It now appeared that James was losing interest in his Ulster lands. The undertakers might have to go in person to see that buildings were completed by the end of the summer. It was now proposed to make a further survey of Ireland to insure future developments in Ulster. Only by this means could the serious colonisers be separated from the planters who had little enthusiasm.

Lord Deputy Chichester had not envisaged beginning his new survey until the middle of the summer of 1613. King James wanted this done as soon as possible, but it actually took place between 2 February and 25 April 1613. Sir Josias Bodley was in charge. He had served the English Crown in Ireland almost continuously since 1598. He had been in charge of the 1609 survey. On 3 December 1612 he was appointed director general of fortification in Ireland.

Bodley's survey is considered much more important than Carew's. He spent a total of seventy-nine days in the escheated counties, as opposed to only thirty-one days spent in 1611. Bodley took considerable time getting information compiling his observations. He relied heavily upon the sheriffs' generous reports. Bodley visited the colonised lands himself. It appears that Bodley's survey was carried out by Bodley himself rather than by a number of commissioners.

As director general of fortifications he went into detailed account of bawns, castles and other buildings erected by the planters. He could report on these without any exterior help. To complete the duties he had to rely upon the landowners but there are indications that Bodley thought that some were providing information. Sometimes he distinguished himself between those tenants who actually held land and those who held titles to it. Bodley was careful how he extracted information, using the phrase "as I understand" to qualify his observations. His estimates of population seem to be reasonably reliable. Sometimes he could be vague, but his report is first class in comparison to Carew's. The result of Bodley's survey had confirmed James's suspicion that certain undertakers had expanded their estates by incorporating the less fortunate planters. Eight Scottish plantations had changed hands completely, and two others remained in Scottish hands. Abercorn had taken over Sir Thomas Boyd's importations in Strabane, while Sir James Craig, as well as owning land in Armagh, had acquired the 2,000 acres in County Cavan. The plantation grew in strength. It was estimated, according to Carew's figures, that in the autumn of 1611 the Scots population of the escheated counties ranged between 350 and 700 adults. This number doubled over the next eighteen months and may have increased considerably. As regards Bodley, there is no evidence to show that all the planters had come from Scotland. In two cases he showed that some Englishmen had settled on Scots-owned land. Estimates of the number of Scots in Ulster in King James I's reign are uncertain. In 1613, with the exception of Strabane, the Scots elements in the town are not included. In seven out of seventeen towns in the escheated counties, most of which had been incorporated in 1613 or 1614, there are a considerable number of Scots names. The number of Scots in the various towns must have varied a lot, and no clear pattern of their presence can be established; Clogher in County Tyrone was the only town where all the burgesses had Scottish names. As far as the Church of Ireland was concerned, the Scots were mainly Presbyterian in origin. Elsewhere the Scots were in the minority, and in Carew's day were mainly confined to the towns, which were either on the coast or accessible to it. However, the number of Scots in these towns is hard to estimate. It has been estimated that 1,400 to 1,500 Scots had colonised the escheated counties by the beginning of 1613.

Except in the towns, the Scots remained on the lands assigned to them. Most of the settlement had taken place in Tyrone, Donegal and Armagh. Armagh contained only one Scottish precinct or barony as opposed to two in the other counties; the situation here was as effective as in Donegal. In Armagh most of the Scots existed because of the efforts of one man. In County Tyrone the land belonged to Abercorn and his brother, Sir George, and this accounts for the presence of 170 of the 224 families present. Since 1611 the greater advance in colonisation had taken place in Donegal. Three men by 1611 had brought with them many tenants. Others brought with them three or four families. The general trend was for the increase in the British presence in the county. Three other undertakers besides Abercorn and Sir George Hamilton had made progress in the Strabane area in regard to tenants. Others abandoned the struggle. The chief undertaker of the Donegal plantation was Lord Ochiltree, but he had let his efforts flag, and no additional families were settled in the region. Only in Sir Robert Hepburn's region had colonisation continued to flower. In Armagh progress was slow. On one piece of land the British population had declined since 1611. On a second count the population had increased only slightly. On a third proportion there seems to have been a complete turnover in the British population. Bodley had described the population as just having arrived from Scotland. Settlement had not ceased in counties Cavan and Monaghan, but the general trend was to the establishment of a prosperous plantation. There was one outstanding exception to this failure: Sir Alexander Hamilton had thirty-six Scots and Englishmen hard at work erecting buildings.

The situation in Fermanagh was the most contradictory. The number of British settlers in the two Scottish baronies in Fermanagh only barely exceeded those in Donegal. None of the colonisers had been successful, but few had entirely failed. Little or no progress had been made on Lord Burley's estate, which had shown great promise in 1611. In other places the number of British had declined since the previous survey. In Sir George Carew's survey a lot of land had passed into English hands, and of those remaining only three were the most successful, containing only four or five families. The Scots were busy erecting buildings; the work of some nineteen to twenty Scots. In this respect Fermanagh's record was better than that of Donegal's where many buildings had been erected. It was the Tyrone development that shone out, whilst the record of County Cavan was the worst. Four Scots had built mills in an effort to cut down costs. The emphasis was upon erecting stone houses and bawns, cemented with lime and clay.

The most spectacular advance in building since 1612 had been made by Sir John Howe in Fermanagh. At the start of the plantation activities he had no buildings on his land, but by 1613 he had erected a stone castle three storeys high, and he had started to build a stone wall to surround and defend his bawn. The colonisers that were most ahead of their time were

Abercorn and his brother Sir George Hamilton. As mentioned in a previous chapter, Abercorn had been permitted to draw twenty-five men from the Irish army for his assistance. However, it is not clear how this would take place. Abercorn maintained the right to impress any ship on the west coast of Scotland in order to bring provisions and supplies to Ulster. In August 1614 Abercorn had received a letter from King James, even though he had not completed his planting, releasing him from the more immediate plans for the Scots colonising in the northern Ulster counties.

As far as Sir George Hamilton was concerned he asked for no favours, but he may have been able to rely upon his brother as far as the importance of shipping was concerned. The success of Abercorn and his brother was due to their determination to colonise and plant Gaelic land. No other Scots received similar favours, and success amongst the planters must have been due to the individual character of the colonisers.

There were problems inhibiting the progress of the Scots presence in Ulster, for as we have seen the Scots found it hard to raise the capital required for plantation purposes. Some of the Scots realised quite quickly a return on their investment. The problem of how to raise cash came to a head by 1615. Lord Ochiltree could not achieve anything between the dates of the two surveys put forward for the plantation of Ulster. By 1613 he was in serious financial difficulties. By 1615 he had to sell his eastern Scots estates along with his Scottish title. However, Ochiltree's plight was not unusual; but in Ochiltree's case he had led an expedition to the Isles in order to set up an Ulster-style plantation. Costs (e.g. transport) were rising, and part of Ochiltree's predicament may have arisen because of this. By 1612 the cost of transportation had been extremely high, and Abercorn and other undertakers had to protest about this to the Scottish Council. They said that for success in Ulster it was essential that there should be easy movement of livestock and men. He put forward the idea of modernising the ferry system to the province. The ship owners had threatened not to ship cargoes and had raised freight rates. The Council ordered the justice of the peace to look into the matter, but there were no more complaints, so the issue may have been settled to the satisfaction of either party. Nothing is known to us of the ship owners' argument, and Abercorn was liable to complain even if there was no jurisdiction. The Scots were extremely cautious about the spending of money. Even if a coloniser had plenty of money his position could be undermined by land disputes with his neighbours. The English government at this point was anxious that disputes between undertakers and the Ulster farmers could cause trouble. In an attempt to avoid trouble the English privy council gave the Irish lord deputy and the plantation commissioners in 1610 power to settle any difference that might come about. The position was full of complications and nothing positive could be done overnight.

The cartographers had made a great contribution to the plantation plans in 1609, but some thought that there were errors and omissions. The same balliboe was sometimes granted to two separate patentees. It was difficult to identify disputes immediately. The undertakers had to occupy lands for months before they could credibly put forward ideas, e.g. proposals for expansion on Irish land. The first dispute involving the Scots arose in April 1611 at which time complaints were being made to King James and the English Council. There were three men that complained that land was rightfully theirs. The Scots made their representation via London in the hope that the administration at Dublin would come out in favour of them. The methods achieved a measure of success, but at this point James was unwilling to interfere. However, Lord Deputy Chichester regarded the situation as being impossible to resolve, so he referred the situation back to London.

Carew now arrived in Ireland, and he brought with him authority to resolve disputes. Other commissioners journeyed north and they ignored the various complaints that had arisen. Thirty-seven instances of differences emerged between landowners; approximately one third of these were Scots. The commissioners dismissed a minor dispute made by Sir James Craig in Armagh as frivolous. In another case they declared that the commission had received their instructions — it mentioned 199 cases, which only involved twelve per cent of the Scots. Such a small number might suggest that the Scots played an important role, but they remained relatively unembroiled. The twenty-four cases concerned eighteen men, or nearly half the number of Scots who had made an effort to settle on their estates in the first year. Disputes seemed to have inhibited the colonising of Scots in Ulster. In 1612 the commissioners stated that settlement of the undertakers' differences would expedite the fulfilment of the conditions, and there are many instances that corroborate this view. There is the example of Claud Hamilton of Creichness, who had established a rich colony at Armagh by the end of the summer of 1611. Whilst he was in the middle of building, his neighbour, Robert Maxwell, Dean of Armagh, laid claim to five and a half of his balliboes, upon one of which stood Hamilton's semi-completed buildings. The claims of the commissioners were endorsed by King James. Bodley found no building had taken place on the proportion from the time the Dean of Armagh had made his complaints.

The settlement made by King James I led to disruption in the colonisation process, but there were also more cases where the plan for the plantation and colonisation were made on difficult ground. James had sent instructions to the lord deputy in 1611 to encourage Lord Burley in any case or dispute with his neighbour, Conor Roe Maguire, the foremost landowner in County Fermanagh. Royal intervention did nothing to end this dispute. By 1612 the size of the dispute reached beyond the capabilities of the local press in Ulster. The matter was referred to the Council, but a year passed and nothing had been done. Also, in Donegal, the land question gave rise to disputes.

No building had been erected by 1613 on the lands belonging to Sir James Cunningham and his uncle. The lack of development can be attributed to disputes with the servitors, who held patents in regard to land before the disputes. The same servitor refused to hand over land granted to Alexander McAulay, for in this case as well he had land granted by King James. The king wrote to Chichester, the lord deputy, about the subject, saying McAulay and his tenants were deprived of the best part of their plantation. Another problem confronting the colonisers was Ulster's wild terrain. Physical conditions very often stood in the way of relations between prospective landlords and Gaelic peasants.

It was not only Ulster that was in a backward state, for the west coast of Scotland was a region of great political challenges. This may have demoralised many of the planters. Conditions on the land had declined as a result of natural calamities and the Scots ran the risk of losing their belongings and investments. Abercorn required large ships to bring about work in the Scottish Isles and the Ulster coast. Planters who were not as rich as Abercorn ran the risk of losing their lives in more ordinary vessels. Even if the passage was without incident there was plenty of risk of danger in remote Ulster. Disembarkation from the ships could also cause trouble. In 1635 one traveller said that in order to land his own horses in Island Magee (where Ochiltree had also landed livestock in 1611), the planters had to dive into the waters and make their way ashore. The rugged nature of the Ulster colony now lay before the planters. In 1613 Chichester had said that it was little different from before. The outlying regions of the plantation were the least developed. By about 1620 an English servitor complained that his holding in a part of County Tyrone was in a bad condition. Building suffered as physical obstacles stood in the way of expansion. Timber had to be fetched from as far as twenty-four miles away, whilst the stones for the walls had to be hauled twelve miles over *filthy and boggy mountains.*

The Gaels of Ulster would be considerably affected by the Scottish colonisers as well as Gaels in the most poor regions. The Gaels deeply resented the coming of the Scots, for they were put out of house and home. They were always under pressure to change their way of life and become more Scots and English. In 1611 an Irishman appeared before the judges for threatening to kill one of the undertakers and throw his head out of the window of his own castle. The Gaels boasted that the exiled Earl of Tyrone would return and drive the Scots and English out of the country. The Gaels had to resort to breaking the law in order to support themselves. Chichester claimed in 1614 that he had seen the departure of 6,000 swordsmen to fight for Sweden, but this did not diminish the position of the Gaels of Ulster. The Scots lived in constant dread of an Irish uprising, and the Irish hated the Scots more than the English.

In March 1611 the Scottish Council heard a complaint that a Scot and his wife, who had gone to settle in County Down, were stripped of all valuables by a band of Gaels led by one Rowland Savage, a descendant of the Norman settlers. In 1612 Sir James Douglas, the chief Scottish undertaker at Armagh, complained to King James that he and his fellow-planters had become discouraged by the Irish risings. It was found that there were more frequent threats from the Irish. The Gaels would remain on the land if the colonisers took a favourable attitude to colonising. The threat of robbery and crime discouraged the Scots planters at Armagh. A year later Bodley conducted his survey and Sir James Douglas handed responsibilities for his lands and proportions over to his neighbour, Henry Acheson.

The Irish made an important impression upon the planters. A report had been made by Lord Deputy Chichester in 1615 after he had visited eastern Tyrone and Londonderry. The planters were confronted by some forty wood kern, as the Gaels were called. In some parts the planters had ceased all building, and the undertakers threatened to return to the place they had come from. These outlaws were robbing in the early 17th century, but they could never threaten the colonisers as a whole. There was of course the continued threat of the outlaws and Chichester was critical and moved to chastise the planters. He found that the original settlers had not completed their side of the plantation bargain. They were open to rebellion by the Irish. It was proposed that a body of soldiers should always be ready in England should the situation in Ulster get out of hand. The fear was not without foundation, for later in 1612 Sir John Wishart, a Scot who had lands in Fermanagh, got wind of what might be a conspiracy. Chichester investigated the matter and he could only report back that nothing untoward had happened or was to happen. He had a general desire to get rid of the undertakers. In the spring of 1615 a plot was discovered which had existed for three years. The 1615 conspiracy was the work of two men, both of whom claimed that they had been deprived of their original inheritance. The first conspirator was Alexander MacDonnell, eldest son of James MacDonnell and nephew of Sir Randal MacDonnell. Sir Randal claimed that he should have had the ownership of the MacDonnell lands after his father's death in 1601. The second conspirator was Rory O'Cahan, who did not like Sir Thomas Phillips for capturing his father after the O'Doherty rising, and for afterwards gaining O'Cahan's castle at Limavady. There was to be an attack upon Coleraine, Londonderry and other British settlements. Tyrone's bastard son, who was a prisoner at Charlemont fort, was to be released. Important Englishmen were captured to be made hostages, the rest being slaughtered.

The Antrim MacDonnells were involved in the Ulster disputes and it was hoped that soldiers would be brought over from the Isles to support British efforts in the province. They expected support from one or two Lowland Scots in Ulster. Brian Crossagh O'Neill assured his fellow-conspirators that one William Stewart (who had married his sister) would campaign for the Scots of the Isles. The Scots should be spared from any general massacre, but the scheme was badly contrived in nearly every detail. It was expected that the Scottish landowners might turn against their English neighbours. It is not sure who William Stewart was, but it is likely that his achievements were no idle boast. There is no evidence to show that any important Lowland Scots knew about the plot before Dublin Castle uncovered it. It was to be a long time before the plotters could attack the Scots colonisers. The government in Ireland discovered what was happening and arrested most of the ringleaders. There was some support for the uprising from the Scots but this did not prevent the continual influx of Scots into Ulster. This was the only uprising that took place in the reign of King James I after 1610. There was great discontent amongst the Irish during the early years of the colony.

It was planned that the Scots should turn against the English, but the plan had little success. There was traditionally very little contact between the Scots and the English. These were crucial years. Chichester regarded it as important that he should encourage relations between both Scots and English for which King James was eternally grateful. The Scots, when they made complaints, bypassed the lord deputy and approached James first, a practice that Chichester did not like. There was one case of a Scot and the deputy having a difference of opinion, but apart from this the plantation of Ulster got off to a quiet start. The Dublin administration oversaw the difference between Scots and Irish, but felt that there was no case for interfering. The Scots petitioned a second clerk of the Irish Council. Those who were approached should be able to read and write but they felt their position was either being misunderstood or not heard at all.

There was hostility between Scots and Irish. Abercorn's brother said that Lord Audley, an Englishman, had spoken out against the Scottish nation during disputes over land with the earl. Audley denied the charges and said that some of Abercorn's men had threatened his life, but he said that the earl had no complicity in the threat. Another event of ill-feeling between Scots and Irish occurred when Sir James Douglas implied that servitors at Armagh had taken part in Irish robberies. These Anglo-Irish welcomed any ill-fortune that might attend the Scots. The servitors complained that the Scots had increased the extent of their livestock. These petty incidents did not threaten the Scottish settlement, and jealousies among the undertakers only helped to lower the tone of the colonisation.

There was difficulty in the Scots travelling to Ulster, for there was a controversy about their legal status. The Crown had as yet to assert its rights over the lands of the two earls and their legal status could not be established until the Act of Attainder made a declaration. The legal position of all the earls was in question until the act was passed. To formalise the Scots practice the Irish parliament was called between 1613 and 1615.

The insecurity of the land position affected both Scots and English. The act prohibiting the Scots entering Ireland had still been in force in Queen Mary's reign. The act affecting the Scots and the Irish was finally repealed in 1615. The discriminating legislation passed in England did not materially affect the Scots position in Ireland. The planters were no longer regarded as outlaws, but what was now more important was the necessity of obtaining denizenship, with which they qualified to own Irish land. All the original planters had clauses of denizenship included in their contracts, but those who followed them did not qualify for a special position in regard to the land. Many had taken land in freehold without gaining denizenship. Thus in common law their lands could be seized by the Crown. To solve the situation Lord Deputy Chichester suggested the passing of acts of naturalisation for all those involved in the disputes.

The problem was that any act introduced into the Irish parliament first had to have the approval of the English Council. This meant that private bills introduced into the Irish parliament first had to have its approval. Private bills introduced into the Irish parliament were very expensive. Chichester suggested the temporary suspension of Poyning's Law which bypassed this act. The situation was not finally settled until 1634 when an act was passed for the naturalisation of many Scots. The affected colonisers were those born before the accession of King James to the throne.

Absentee landlords were a problem during the plantation years and this had a number of causes. As we have seen, the tendency was for planters to neglect their Ulster duties. If an undertaker died, this usually posed a problem about absentees. The colonisers had fallen into disgrace — a fate worse than death. Lord Burley fell into disfavour between November 1612 and April 1613 for opposing a grant made by the Crown to the Scottish parliament. This was one of the reasons why the process of the plantation took so long. Burley eventually came into royal favour again, but never again was he interested in Ulster events. The articles of plantation had stated that at least ten British families, for every acre granted, had to be on the proportion by November 1611. The Scots had achieved 81,000 acres. By this time 800 families should have put down roots on Gaelic soil. Burley pointed out the presence of just over half that number of families in 1613. The plantation demanded all transactions should have been carried out by May 1614. There was only a year left in which to carry out the government's proposals. Many of the Scots had not completed their terms of the agreement, and had shown little interest in the initial state of the plantation. Sixteen proportions remained unfounded and little work was done for eighteen months. The official survey was very disappointed about the position in Ulster. High expenses, disputes over territory, rugged conditions and other problems had weighed down the proposals of the British effort. The proposals set forward at the foundation of the plantation were unrealistic, and the Scots fell well short of King James's plans for the colonisation of the nine counties of Ulster. The plantation, however, had moved forward at a slow pace. In 1611 there were thirty-three to thirty-seven proportions with some settlement. By 1613 there were forty-three. The Scots, though, had doubled their population between the taking of the two surveys, and the general movement was for the Protestant population of the province to slowly increase. If the Scots were not too firmly established, if more and more proportions joined those with a static or declining immigrant population, the entire scheme for a Scots Ulster might pass away. If the Scottish population increased on the land, it would serve to be a rule in the development of Ulster. The fate of the Scots position in the nine counties was as yet to be decided.

Chapter 8

A Firm Foundation

The Scots efforts did not die out after the early years for there was great determination. Several years after Bodley had completed his work, the pace of the colonisation seems to have gathered strength. The survey was not to be until the end of 1618. There is a lack of detail exploring the position in Ulster between 1613 and 1619. But there was an influx of Scots into Ulster between 1615 and 1617. In the precinct of Portlough, forty-one men became the tenants of James Montgomery's proportion. In June the following year William Stewart of Dunduff leased land to a number of British tenants, almost all of them Scots; five months later there was a further colonisation by the Donegal Cunninghams. Three or four proportions contained as many tenants at the time of either Carew's or Bodley's survey. A lot of information can be gleaned from the number of Scots obtaining denizenship.

There were the original Scots in Ulster, but only fifteen Scots became denizens in Ireland between 1611 and 1614. Many of these were those that had settled outside of the escheated counties. Between 1615 and 1617 a large number of lands were granted to the Scots — the number rising from 336 — the peak year being 1617 when 180 were issued. New measures had been introduced in 1615 governing the denizenship procedure. The Irish parliament did not help the Scots in their quest for naturalisation. King James decreed that in the future up to forty names might be included on the denizenship certificate. The cost for each applicant was substantially reduced. This only partly explains the influx of Scots into Ulster. After 1617 there was a decline in their numbers: in 1618 there was only one, in 1619 there were thirty-eight and after this only a small number. The regulations had not been changed. The increase in numbers arose not only because denizenship had become easier to obtain, but also because there were more people awaiting possession.

The Scots now had word that it was easier to obtain land in Ulster, and that the severity of conditions had declined. The lands had begun to yield revenue, but there were more reports of expensive transport dues; the attacks by the Irish had become less frequent; and even the question of boundaries between estates had become less acute. Another reason why there was an increase of Scots into Ireland was that there was continuous pressure from England, especially from King James, to make the undertakers fulfil their obligations.

Bodley's report had been finished by 1613, but King James ordered that a new one should be made in the autumn of 1614. Little remains of these transactions except parts of Londonderry. A communication from England had prompted Lord Deputy Chichester to write a letter in December 1614: it was suggested that Bodley should come over from England late that year, or early in the next one, carrying with him a fresh survey. James seems to have taken measures to shake the planters out of their laziness. It was stated that the undertakers should erect more buildings. It is unclear the overall purpose of the memorandum. It is possible that King James sent Chichester general instructions on the policy to be adopted against the planters. He complained about the laziness and lethargy of the undertakers. He found that the undertakers were not capable of carrying out their obligations. He informed Chichester that he intended to extend the deadline for the completion of the buildings. This should take place by 31 August 1616. After this deadline he intended to seize the lands. King James admonished Chichester and said that there should be no distinction between Englishmen and Scots in the agreements. Before long the English privy council, in March 1616, ordered Chichester to find out as soon as possible from the Scots and English undertakers the position without making a disturbance in the country. It is not well known how the undertakers were able to defend themselves and how many horse and foot they could obtain. The exercise was not meant to find families for the undertakers, but to assess the power position of the king and his colonisers, particularly in Ulster. There does not seem to be any evidence to support these reports, but later that year another survey was conducted. Sir Oliver St John had succeeded Chichester as lord deputy in August. King James let St John know that he wanted a loyal and extensive plantation in Ulster and the rest of Ireland. He wanted the Earl of Abercorn to fall heir in the Strabane region and to build where there were only crude buildings before. The deputy had given the planters a royal grant for those who were not carrying out their obligations despite warnings.

Many looked forward to Bodley's survey, but little of it has survived except one part conducted in November 1614. The survey that looked beyond Londonderry became the survey of 1618-1619, occasionally comparing the Ulster plantation with those in the rest of Ireland. Bodley reported in the negative about the conditions at Londonderry. Another feature of the letter of St John was the grant given to Abercorn. The Scottish bonds remained in Edinburgh, and James sent another letter to his Scottish

Council giving it permission to acquire the Strabane bonds of Abercorn. In the previous year it was unable to pay its debts of £30,000 (Scots) but this may have been only one way of settling the account. The plan may have been implemented to keep out Britain's greatest coloniser in Ireland. This appears to be the motive behind the Baron of Strabane's title to his estates. It was more likely intended to combine a favour to the earl with a view to frightening the planters into possession of their lands. The plan marked the beginning of punitive measures against the colonisers. Once the deadline was up, King James was anxious to know if the undertakers had kept their promise.

King James visited Scotland in the previous year and problems in religious quarters diverted his attention away from Ulster. He returned to his task in Ulster in 1618 to make sure that the colonisers were properly planting the lands. At the end of March he ordered St John to inform the planters that as he had heard bad reports about them he was going to draw them to serious account. A survey was ordered for that summer. The report asserted that it would not have any arrogance on the planters' side. Some of the measures were implemented during that summer, but without success. Some of the bonds of the undertakers were dispatched to Ireland in order that it might be ascertained which of the planters had broken bond. However, by December some of the Scots had not reached Dublin. A survey was conducted of the number of men at arms in Ulster, but the survey lacked authority over the planters. A proclamation was issued declaring that all Irish land was to be British land by 1 May 1619. Other orders in the past like this were ignored with impunity and there was no motivation to obey the king. Nothing had been achieved that summer, but preparations were under way on 28 November. Captain Nicholas Pynnar received the commission to size up the situation.

Pynnar had been in Ireland since 1600 and had received land in Ulster, though he did little to develop it. He spent 119 days in Ulster compiling his report — much more than Bodley, who took seventy-nine days in 1613. As a result of the extended time, Pynnar was able to provide more detail than the other reports. He described the buildings and often the state of agriculture. He listed numbers of freeholders, and the total number of men at arms and their families. He also noted the numbers of planters that had taken the Oath of Supremacy. Pynnar visited most of the proportions personally, and he treated with great care information provided to him by the undertakers. There was the case of Sir John Hume in Fermanagh, who said that there was a number of men nominated as freeholders that were not resident upon the land. Others appealed to Pynnar about the abuse they were receiving at the hands of the landlords. He was not an undertakers' spokesman. Pynnar took great care in compiling his report, but it must be treated with caution when it is used as a measure for the Scottish colonisation. His statistics of British males were ascertained, but these totals must be treated with care. Pynnar concluded that in the six counties that he surveyed he might be able to raise up to 2,000 more British men than he had listed. His estimate for Portlough, a Scottish precinct in Donegal, fell far short of the true number. In 1622 134 British men could be raised and were described by Pynnar as being loyal subjects. Of the male totals it is likely that Pynnar erred on the side of caution.

There was the problem of separating Scots from British before the advent of the surveyors. Pynnar's survey shows a tendency for Englishmen to acquire land and for the Scots to become landowners beyond their own estimates. By 1619 eight of the proportions had passed into English hands. At Knockninny only one Scottish landlord remained. The Scots leased out land in areas which had been earmarked for them. It seems that the majority of the Scots leased out their land according to the survey of 1618-1619. By 1619 there seems to be some intermingling between Scots and English tenants. There is little evidence that there was less likelihood for Scots to settle on English land. Lord Audley, an English servitor, claimed that in 1614 rent was paid by both English and Scots. By 1616 only half of the English in Donegal possessed English names. There is no evidence that the Scots settled with a majority of Englishmen. Pynnar was vague on the position about nationalities — the word British was his description of the colonists. However, relatives were mostly Scots. It was recommended that all Scots settling on English land should come from Scotland. However, there were Scots living on English lands which had been omitted from the survey.

There was an increase in Scots in one part of County Cavan between 1613 and 1619, the result of pressure of population in Scotland; County Cavan being one of the nine counties of Ulster. Bodley found that there was nothing to be done on the estate acquired by Sir James Hamilton of Clandeboye from Lord Aubigny. Pynnar reported a total of forty-one British families who could muster eighty armed men.

From the survey of 1622 we know that the tenants were Scots in origin, but most of them had come from Hamilton's estate in County Down and not directly from their homeland in Scotland. In the two eastern counties of Antrim and Down there was some movement to the other seven counties in the province. It would be impossible to calculate the extent of the migration between 1613 and 1619. So James's method seems to be unique for he was the only Scot living apart from the migration of Scots being assessed.

Since 1613 there had been a definite increase in the British population of Scots-owned territory. In financial terms County Tyrone was the best settled, but Armagh had only a small Scots population and it takes second place. Neither Cavan nor Fermanagh had large English and Scots estates, but they were not as impressive as the position in County Donegal in 1613. The British population in Donegal had increased since 1613 but at a slow rate. Between 1613 and 1619 the total British adult population on Scottish estates had been doubled. The population increased during a five-year period — about the same as during the eighteen months between Carew's and Bodley's surveys. The rate of growth had declined but the 140 adults on Sir James Hamilton's estates in Cavan have been excluded from the 1619 total. The movement from Scotland to Ulster between 1613 and 1619 was very considerable. By 1619 the Scots in the escheated counties exceeded the 5,500 mark, but sources are unreliable — the 1619 situation suggests that 300 would be a conservative estimate.

The Scots had settled their lands between 1613 and 1619, which can be attributed to the half-hearted efforts of other planters and their replacement by more capable Scots. It is not true that when a Scot gave up his land he left Ireland and Ulster. Sir John Wishart of Pittarro stayed on after to become some years later an aid to the Bishop of Clogher. James MacCullough and Alexander Cunningham continued to live on their lands after settling them. The duties of undertakers now passed to others. During the first three years of the plantation, nine proportions changed hands. During the next six years the rate of turnover about doubled. During this period thirty-two acres of land acquired new owners; eight going to English men already mentioned. By 1619 only eighteen of the original male landowners or their spouses remained in control. In Cavan and Fermanagh these lands to some extent were open to plantation. The first plantation remained under the direction of the original patentees, but collapsed at the end of the first year, and was taken over by other colonisers who would make a second attempt, guided by a group of new men. Only four of the original twenty-two colonised participated in the new regime. The estates grew in size as a result of changing hands. Some settlers did not own Irish land. The leading planters already had Ulster lands before making larger plantations. By 1613 a concentration of landlords had taken place in the north. By the time of Bodley's survey Henry Acheson had acquired Sir James Douglas's lands in Armagh.

Sir James Craig, a second Armagh Scot, had taken over the two proportions in County Cavan, and Abercorn had acquired Sir Thomas Boyd's land in Strabane. By 1619 the colonisation was in full swing. A man and his family planted and extended their land. In Armagh John Hamilton, brother of Sir James Hamilton of Clandeboye, possessed great lands, and he also owned land in County Cavan. In Mountjoy, Robert Stewart was replaced by Lord Ochiltree's son and replaced by Robert Stewart of Hilton. In Strabane Sir George Hamilton administered the estate of his dead brother. In Portlough, Sir James Cunningham took over Cunningham's original grant, and Sir John Hume had taken over William Fowler's grant in Magheraboy.

The modification of the plantation scheme went under way, with the intention of keeping the lands of the smaller colonisers. At Boylagh and

Banagh John Murray, groom to the king's bedchamber, royal favourite and later to become an earl, was granted the entire barony. The tendency was to increase the proportions in a piecemeal manner and usually with King James's blessing. Let us look at the history of the barony between 1613 and 1619. Bodley, the surveyor, had found little progress in Boylagh and Banagh despite the absence of the chief planters. Nothing had been achieved between the above dates and the coming of Pynnar. In 1619 Boylagh and Banagh were the least densely populated, but it contained the second largest number of population. In this barony it had been the tendency for undertakers to rent out their lands to others, but the first two surveys took no notice of the situation. Four of the lands had been sold or rented by early 1613.

The authorities were dissatisfied with the progress made when the barony was split up. James agreed to let Sir Robert Gordon of Lochinvar buy out the original owners. Gordon was a wealthy laird or lord of Kirkcudbrightshire. At one time he was associated with an income of £1,000 sterling per annum. James was of the opinion that such resources at his command would be able to make a Scots settlement in this desolate barony thrive vigorously. There was the question of what Gordon's title would be. It was not certain but, whatever his intention, in August Gordon bought his first two proportions. Three months later he received a grant to the whole barony, and in 1615 he bought more land. Gordon was unable to fulfil the conditions made with James about the land, so that by October 1618 the king had decided to grant the barony to John Murray. Murray had played a role in the barony long before its owner. George Murray of Brighton was his closest kinsman and he probably obtained the title of landowner through his position at court. John Murray wrote to the Scottish Secretary of State that he would faithfully carry out his instructions, but he died in August 1613. According to his widow, the terms of the plantation were not carried out. There were to be great efforts to obtain lands; John Murray appears to have obtained a grant of land for Sir Robert, but this is impossible to prove. John Murray retained an everlasting love of Ulster in these pioneering years. In October 1616 he obtained lands in Donegal from Sir Robert McClelland.

James issued instructions in October 1616 for the barony to be granted to John Murray but the terms of the grant showed considerable change. Murray himself and all his tenants were to receive denizenship. To rectify the problem of the boundaries between lands, a commission was established to examine all the titles to land and to incorporate all changes. Murray intended to carry out elaborate plans to build a settlement, to be called Murraystown, and he was to be granted a charter for it at his request. The soil of Boylagh and Banagh was barren and the plantation was almost remote. King James thought about tinkering with the situation, but this did not materialise. The original grants had been insufficient in some way, probably in regard to denizenship. The natural increase in estates' size was not necessary to the scheme. James had granted entire baronies first to Gordon and then to Murray. The king considered that the plantation in Down had been well established before 1610. This plantation was more sophisticated than any other in the province.

The situation in Boylagh and Banagh indicates some of the features of the Scots plantation. One man — Sir Robert McClelland — was the leading light in these years of colonisation. He reveals how it was to be a Scot setting up his colony on Gaelic soil in Ulster. More information exists than about any other of the plantations. Sir Robert had not obtained his majority when King James granted him lands at Rossee in Donegal. He had already made his mark upon the political situation. By 1610 he had been committed to court twice for assault and had been involved in a family feud with the Gordons of Lochinvar. However, he had made no effort to colonise his Donegal lands. Carew and Bodley found them unsettled, but he did not forsake his interest in Ulster. In 1614 he married Sir Hugh Montgomery's eldest daughter, who had a considerable dowry of several townlands in County Down. McClelland leased his Donegal lands to Archibald Acheson, a brother of Henry Acheson of Armagh. Nevertheless both McClelland and Archibald Acheson disposed of their Donegal estates to join John Murray.

A few months before the above events, Sir Robert first showed an interest in renting lands belonging to the Haberdashers' Company in Londonderry. On 30 May 1616, Adrian Moore, one of the members of the company who was responsible for the British estates in Ireland, wrote to one of the Irish Society's agents in Ulster saying that McClelland was very much interested in the Haberdashers' proportion. Sir Robert had agreed to pay 8d sterling per acre, excepting wood and bog which amounted to £400 sterling for all the lands. He agreed to carry out the company's obligations on the proportions. The two parties came to some agreement, but at this stage there arose the issue of the Society's security of payment of rent.

McClelland did not give up as a result of these setbacks. He sent agents to look at the Haberdashers' lands. There was a favourable report and he complained to James that Moore refused to negotiate. James handed the matter over to the English Lord Chancellor, and by August, after much debate, an agreement was reached. The lease was to last fifty-one years and the rent was settled at £350 10s 0d sterling per annum. To insure payment of the rent for the first three years, Sir Robert had to agree to pay £1,000 by 25 December 1616, although the lease was not to begin till 1 May 1617. Until the £1,000 sterling was paid, the articles of agreement were to remain in the hands of the Keeper of the Tower, Sir George Moore. To guarantee the payment of rent in further years, McClelland and two friends had to agree to pay a bond of £2,000 sterling as security. Now the Haberdashers had to complete the stone house, already started on the new lands by the time McClelland took up residence. The agreement was modified and it was discovered that three years' rent (as had been originally agreed) was not enough. Sir Robert was to find it difficult to raise the £1,000. He paid £100 on 24 December 1616, and Moore accepted this on the condition that the remainder should be paid as soon as possible.

Sir Robert stayed in London until events in Ulster started to hot up. King James, in March, wrote a letter on his behalf, instructing the lord deputy to grant denizenship to the Scots that had arrived in Londonderry as a result of the lease. In April the indenture to the lease was secured. As the Haberdashers had promised to pay Sir Robert such a large sum they found it impossible to meet their obligation, and Sir Robert was to receive £60 to pay for the completion. Moore wrote to the agent in Ireland urging full cooperation with the new leasee. By the end of April Sir Robert was on his way from London, visiting Scotland first and then continuing to Ireland. Before the Scots were able to settle on the Haberdashers' land, those in County Londonderry were mainly confined to the Tower. George Montgomery drew some Scots to County Londonderry when he was bishop of the city, but he was shortly to be transferred to the sees of Meath and Clogher in 1610. Those Scots who had colonised Ulster before the setting up of the plantation were lucky to survive. Sir Robert was to set up his own plantation there fifteen years later, and he wrote to complain that Londonderry was a most hostile part of the kingdom, subject to insurrection, robbery and murder. Men of quality could not travel around without an armed guard. The City of London was to be granted the county and a few Scots were to settle the lands between 1610 and 1617. George Canning, the Ironmongers' agent, noted that some of the English and Scots were willing to negotiate with him. The Scots were willing to pay higher rents than the English, although they were slow in erecting the essential buildings. The numbers involved were small. By 1616 only thirteen English and Scottish families had settled in the Ironmongers' proportion. There was little incentive to colonise the county. Like the other undertakers, the City companies did not like long leases, because the value of the land was likely to rise. There was an atmosphere of rebellion (the conspiracy of 1615) and the situation was not conducive for settling. The winter of 1614-1615, according to George Canning, was so severe that many cattle died of starvation in the snow. These conditions were not favourable for an influx of settlers from Scotland into the City lands. As we have seen, the Scots that settled in Ulster were drawn there by the colonisers that were prepared to put up with poor conditions.

Sir Robert wanted his tenants at Londonderry to take up two sections along the eastern bank of the River Roe; one piece of land belonging to the Irish and one to the Church. 23,000 English acres made up the estate, half of which was very good ground, suitable for corn, meadow and pastureland. The rest was mountainous with woods and bogs. By July

1613 a total of £3,124 sterling had been spent on the project, but this large outlay achieved very little. It was difficult to attract tenants and settlers from England. However, by 1616 few of the companies had any degree of success. The Haberdashers' cloth workers, most of whom had come from Scotland, were said to be the most slack. McClelland began operations with the Haberdashers, and had begun negotiations in 1617 with the cloth workers to lease their property. This adjoined the northern section of the land that had already been leased. It stretched east to the River Bann, and lay just across the river from Coleraine. By 1618 he had signed the lease for the new lands and moves were made to settle it with tenants. But almost at once McClelland fell into trouble. He had to pay three years' rent in advance and had to pay £200 for the transporting of eighty to one hundred persons whom he had persuaded to settle on his most recently acquired land. These colonisers must have come after Pynnar had completed his survey, as he found no British on the lands. When the tenants arrived they were told that they would obtain smaller plots of land than they had expected. McClelland had promised them land, thinking it was measured in Irish acres. He discovered that the lands given to him by the cloth workers used smaller English acres as a measure. As a result of this mistake, many colonisers left and returned to their homelands. Those that remained appealed to the lord deputy to have their rents reduced, taking into account the size of the acres. This meant that their landlord not only lost much of the money he had spent in transporting men over to Ireland, but also collected less rent than had been anticipated. To cap it all he lost a land dispute with the Church and some servitors. This meant that he had to pay £55 per annum. As a result some landlords left their lands in fear that rents would go up and that they could not afford to pay. There were attacks made by the Irish. Just as the troubles were seeming to go away, some of his British tenants discovered they could obtain cheaper land on the lands of the other companies. However, Sir Robert's complaint cannot be regarded as a reliable source. It was planned to reduce the rent. By 1622 the cloth workers' land was the second-best planted area in the county of Londonderry. It contained eighty-six men. The first and largest estate was that of Sir Robert, leased from the Haberdashers. His position was unique; he seems to have had a large share of difficulties for a person of his position. Sir Robert had to pay a high rent in comparison to the normal sum demanded by King James from his other landlords.

Land disputes could be disastrous for the life of a proportion, and in this respect Sir Robert's experience was little different from that of the other potentates. To persuade the inhabitants of a neighbour's lands to cross a boundary proved a great temptation. The alternative was to persuade potential tenants to cross the Irish Sea and possibly pay their passage. A Scot, writing a letter in 1630, stated that there was great difficulty in securing tenants, but also stated that there were a few good men. The general position of the Londonderry undertakers was the situation that had survived concerning McClelland's finances. In 1620 the rent of the Haberdashers' lands brought in a rent of £126 10s 9d for half a year. Not including the rent that he had to pay himself, his expenses for the same period amounted to £200 6s 0d leaving a deficit of £73 9s 9d. By 1638 the rent from the Haberdashers' lands had increased to over £530 per annum, but during the reign of King James an income of about £230 per annum seems typical. A servitor, complaining in 1622, said he only earned £120 per annum off 2,000 acres. Sir Claud Hamilton of Schawfield's proportion of 2,000 acres in Strabane had high yields for the years 1613, 1614 and 1615. An undertaker could expect to earn on average about £100 per annum for 1,000 acres, as well as what he earned from selling the crops and livestock of lands which he farmed himself.

It is difficult to estimate if Sir Robert's expenses were typical; his main expense was rent. Two successive reductions were made on the Haberdashers' lands in 1622 and 1623, so that by 1623 he was paying only £200, but the burden of the other colonisers was great. By the end of James's reign, Sir Robert was deeply in debt. He was such an unpopular figure in Ulster and in Scotland that his body had to be guarded. In 1625 he spent £4,200 sterling in raising a force to defeat the Spaniards, but he was not compensated by the Crown until 1639. He died in 1639 and he seems to have left his finances in a respectable state. Rents from the Haberdashers' lands had increased. There were some debts that had to be paid. He owed one debt to an Edinburgh merchant, amounting to £2,100 sterling, but his assets could easily pay off the debt and other commitments.

His spending was not exceptional. Ploughing his wheatland cost £1 6s 0d, and shearing his sheep cost £1 6s 0d. There were also numerous small amounts to be paid; for example his travelling expenses. Cutting and bringing in the harvest cost £12 3s 0d — slightly more than the £9 1s 6d paid to a Mr Godfree of London for his daughter's safety. All these expenses a Scottish undertaker might have to meet.

The accounts of Sir George Hamilton for Sir Claud Hamilton of Schawfield's estate over the years 1613-1615, showed total disembursements of £662 3s 8d for three years. The rents for those years amounted to only £637 12s 6d — a deficit. Accounts were also drawn up to settle Sir Claud's estate, and included such items as £90 0s 0d for payment of his brother's debts. It is not certain when these debts were incurred and the record may not be an accurate reflection of the everyday life in a planter's colony. Sir Robert's accounts cover only half a year, and Sir Claud's were drawn up under similar circumstances. Both men agreed that what was left over from rents after all expenses had been paid was not a large sum. This small profit had to pay off the principal, and interest on any capital originally invested — money spent on transport and the construction of buildings — which amounted to between £500 and £1,000 sterling.

The small profit explains much of the behaviour of the colonists. It explains the high casualty rate amongst the original undertakers. James Chapman collected rent from the 2,000 acres he was granted in Strabane, but achieved nothing on its development. In 1614 he sold the investment for £1,400 sterling. Instead of initial struggles during the year Chapman was able to realise his investment after four years, and at the same shed all responsibility. Colonisers that had entered the project at the beginning could either develop the land or sell it. It must have been a temptation to sell straight away, and it is a wonder that most of them did not follow the selling course. The same temptation did not appertain to those who had bought land from the original potentates, for the land had to sit for a while before a profit could be made by selling. There was only a small amount of money to be made by selling, so the Gaelic lands fell into fewer and fewer hands. The income from one estate might be small; the profit to be realised on two or three estates might be large. Land values rose as more planters set up their farms. If a planter had sufficient capital or credit, it was in his interest to buy up land in the early years when prices were relatively low. It also explains why wealthy Scots like John Murray, the Earl of Abercorn and Sir James Hamilton of Clandeboye did most of the buying. Englishmen on the whole possessed more wealth than the Scots.

The year 1619 now began. Many of the smallholders had been bought out; the wealth adding more to the value of their estates. Settlement, however, had continued at a steady pace, so now the Scots were settling widely throughout Ulster. Were the Scots a failure in their planting, or were they a success? Did the Scots fulfil their agreements, or did they surpass the English? By 1619 between thirty-five and forty of the fifty-one estates were still owned by the Scots, but in building their record was not good. They had inadequate defences and the buildings did not comply with the essentials required by 1610 conditions. But the Scots were better than the English in the building of farms and bawns. Land still owned by the Scots contained approximately thirty-nine men per 1,000 acres. In the English precincts there were thirty men per precinct. Only seventy per cent of the Scottish proportions contained some form of defence work. Such construction could be found in eighty-seven per cent of the English estates. The Scots had applied themselves to the immediate needs of the plantation. The English tenants feared that they might be robbed. The Gaels were afraid that they might be thrust off their lands without notice. They had no interest in raising crops which they might not be paid for. By 1619 the Scots were in a strong position in Ulster despite many of their shortcomings in performance.

Chapter 9

Decadence

Immigration to Ulster from Scotland had reached its peak in 1619. By the end of King James's reign this flow into the province had dwindled to a fraction of the 1619 level. The reason for this is made clear by an examination of the survey made of the plantation in the summer of 1622. Altogether from the inception of the plantation there were to be six surveys. It is important to note that by 1622 Ulster was the only theatre of British policy in Ireland. Even as the Ulster plantation proceeded there were talks about establishing a plantation elsewhere in Ireland. Wexford was considered as a possibility, situated on the east coast of what is today Eire (Republic of Ireland). However, the Gaels of Wexford did not like this intrusion into their personal affairs. During 1611 and 1612 patents were issued to undertakers, but these had to be withdrawn because of the native hostilities. Another plan was drawn up in 1614, which was put into effect over the next three years. The government granted undertakers land in Longford and King's County during 1619 and five years later in Leitrim. There were also the Elizabethan plantations in Munster and in Leix and Offaly, which enjoyed prosperity during the peace of King James's reign. Eighteen men had received grants in Wexford, and only one had a Scots name. In Longford and King's County seven out of fifty-one undertakers probably originated from Scotland, and another seven Scots received grants in Leitrim. However, there was no settling of the land by British tenants by 1622. The post-1610 projects had little effect on Scots migration. They felt there was a need for the 1622 survey. The situation in the north was that it was the only Scots effort in Ireland. The government would have to make further investigations and plans.

The lord deputy sent Pynnar's survey to London early in May 1619. He urged King James to punish those that were faulty. James seems to have been in the same frame of mind even before the survey. Edward Wray, one of the king's gentlemen of the bedchamber, was given the right to levy ten shillings from every Irish family still resident on the lands of the planters.

The intention behind the grant was to penalise the Irish and British planters. The king explained three years later that he granted the levy to Edward Wray because he was a capable fellow and he thought he should be rewarded. By August, though, St John had to modify the advice he had given that May. The remedy had not become more dangerous than the disease. St John wrote to James that the Gaels had taken to the mountains, making way for the colonisation by the Scots. On Church and servitor land the Gaels were permitted to hold leases, and they were already quite well off. However, those leasing undertakers' lands had difficulty in finding a place to go. James now called for a fresh committee of inquiry. Those undertakers that had kept their part of the bargain began to feel insecure. James had been patient with the undertakers and he wanted to give the Scots and the English a second chance. If James was willing to invest more money in Ulster favourable conditions might prevail. Some of the colonisers had to double their Crown rent, and this would remove the fear of eviction for the undertakers. This policy was to be extended to everyone. At this time there were no plans to change the nature of the colony. James declared that new grants confirming titles should not release landowners from their former obligations. Now a group of Englishmen, headed by Sir John Fish, and a Scot, Sir James Craig, decided to act with a more elaborate proposal, which considerably changed the nature of the colonisers' obligations. This petition seems to have been presented sometime before autumn 1620. The petition has perished, but a summary of it has survived, as have other references to it. It is possible to reconstruct its contents.

The petitioners declared that they represented a large part of the British undertakers, and they emphasised the success that had already borne fruit on some of the lands. They used Pynnar's survey. There were in existence 107 strong castles and bawns, and there were about 36,000 British planted; 8,000 of these were able to bear arms. Conditions were rigorous and some twenty-three undertakers had withdrawn from the venture. Firstly they requested that new letters patent be presented to them without any forfeiture clause being attached. They agreed to sign a covenant to fulfil the original conditions on those quarters of their land. They requested that the Gaels could stay on if they accepted the Protestant faith. Secondly they said that at least a year should pass for the removal of the Gaels living on land that had been set aside for the British (Scots). Thirdly they wanted to be allowed the right of holding court and fairs and other such special occasions. Finally they wanted their new patents for half the normal fee. In return for all this the rents would be doubled. This would increase King James's revenues by over £1,000 per annum. It would create a precedent for such an increase in rents on further occasions when others wished to confirm their grants.

A committee was set up in Ireland by November 1620, which said that there should be alterations but no modifications were made. It was advised for example that undertakers should be forbidden to use Irishmen as household servants. Irish labour should be restricted to field tasks such as ploughing and ditching. However, there was an important modification — that concessions should be granted to those who had fulfilled the terms of agreement with the government. It was also suggested that there should be a new survey to discover who was qualified to receive a patent on more generous terms.

In February 1621 orders were given to the Irish Attorney General to prepare for new patents to be issued on the undertakers' terms. Some four years later the undertakers were left with the situation where the overall plan had failed. By July 1621 it was still the ambition of the Lord Treasurer, Sir Henry Montague, and of King James, to grant revised patents. A letter to this effect was only rejected by the English Council at a meeting held on 27 July. The king had been consulted about this letter before it was written, for it was drafted in his name, and reflected his deep interest in the Ulster plantation-and-colonisation process, for it was the creation of his own hands. However, independent of the king's wishes it was the Council that decided matters in Ireland, particularly in Ulster. The undertakers were concerned about the duration of their leases. If new patents were issued without a forfeiture clause, this would give the planters time to consolidate their forces. On 25 May the Irish Council delivered a long statement to the English Council on the subject of lands in the Irish estates in general. The continued progress of the Ulster and other plantations was judged by the personal motivation of the planters themselves. The colonisers were there to build, plant with the British and reside upon lands granted by King James. All the undertakers had to fulfil their obligations for otherwise *those that perform well will be lost through the negligence and sloth of their neighbours*. Because there were few planters it was difficult to fill posts. Now the Gaels started to multiply at a great rate and they would eventually provide a formidable force within and without the colonies.

Another survey was now recommended, which would be more orthodox than that which was proposed by the Irish Council. The English were now deeply concerned with the government of Ireland. By the end of May another commission had been set up to investigate the position of the English government, including the position of the established Anglican Church. New officials were exploring the attitude to the Gaels. Now one Cranfield, long experienced in Irish affairs, was making his comeback. Cranfield and an associate of Sir Arthur Ingram had at first competed in 1613; they jointly acquired the farms of the Irish. The lease of the customs passed to Buckley in 1618, and Cranfield continued his share in the profits. Cranfield had now had word that there was to be yet another survey, which the undertakers may not have liked. The British in Ulster remained few. It was remarked how underpeopled were the Irish lands and the colonies. One can have some sympathy about the position and role of the English Council, for it had to await the investigations. Cranfield had not failed, for he still held wide support. It was the delay in securing their tenure that undermined the conditions of the colonisers and their tenants.

In January 1622 Richard Hudson wrote to Cranfield, who was now the Lord Treasurer, thanking him for his appointment to the commission. Preparations must have been in progress well before 1622. On 20 March the commission received its authority, and by the end of April it had taken up residence in Dublin. It was also called upon to investigate far more of the plantations. It had authority to investigate the Church, the legal system, trade and the army. The activities of the commission had power over many matters. It had reported on the state of affairs in contemporary Ulster, with its growing Scots population. In Ulster work was carried on under previous surveyors. Information was gathered in what manner the land should be settled, what buildings had been erected and which men had performed the task. Moreover the commission's work included what work had been done under previous surveyors and what ills they had found. The commission numbered twenty-one persons, but it was decided that seven of these should be in Ulster. The seven split up into teams of two or three men; each team responsible for the collection of information in two of the escheated counties. Notables received authority that they should carry on the investigation. Lord Caulfield and Sir Nathaniel Rich reported on the counties of Tyrone and Armagh, Sir Thomas Phillips and Richard Hudson on Donegal and Londonderry, and Sir James Perrott on counties Cavan and Fermanagh. Some of the notables could speak Irish. By late July or early August the various teams made known their intentions in Ulster, and by 18 September most of the land had returned to Dublin.

Looking at the 1622 survey presents some simple problems. Firstly, the type of information required differed from county to county. In Donegal both numbers of the colonisers were listed for the precinct of Portlough, while at Boylagh and Banagh the tendency was to number them in proportions. The purpose was to present the population in terms of families. Only occasionally were they aware of the British residents in family units. Pynnar's survey now came into its own again. However, a listing of individuals may have proven hard in the early 17th century. There were complications amongst the farmers that were appointed. Much of the information comes from counties Tyrone and Armagh and for no other shire or county. In Donegal a muster was held in 1622 in which the population was listed in accord with nationality — Irish, English and Scots. This information presents the best account of the conditions of the early 17th century. There were many complications.

In Tyrone and Armagh the same method was used for compiling the survey, indicating the number of tenants on the land; the certificates were often checked, although not normally by the commissioners themselves. Comments were made about its accuracy. Two commissions were made responsible for the surveying of these counties, and they favoured their own opinions.

Finally there is a 17th century copy of the document, which is impressive. It remarked particularly on buildings. Reports were now drawn up about the position of the colonists. Its main work was to report on the condition of the planters and the relationships they had with the Gaels, who saw the land being escheated. In County Tyrone the survey documented the position of their colonists.

There were about 300 families in the barony of Strabane at this time. It was the purpose of the commission to find out how many planters had come from Scotland. It had so far been assumed that the Scots landlords appointed Scots tenants. There are records in the documents and the surveying certificates. Most of the colonisers were Lowland Scots, according to many records. But the same was not true of those reported by landowners in the barony. About half of those listed on this certificate had names such as Babbington, Disney and Spencer. Most of these probably came from England. At least twenty families should have been deducted from the British total when calculating the Scottish presence. This gives the rate of two men to a family, a final count showing 270-280 Scottish families in the barony.

Pynnar estimated the same numbers of Scots and Irish in the barony of Strabane three years later. So the Scottish settlement could not afford to grow. There was a net drop in the number of Scots in the province. Within the barony, Abercorn's estates were much larger than the other colonies. The British totals made up two thirds of the total. The commissioners remarked that they represented a successful colonisation. There was no sign of growth. The barony of Strabane could not raise an adequate force to defend the lands. Abercorn had died in 1618 and Strabane languished. Since the death of the first Earl of Abercorn in 1618 landowners checked the condition of their estates. There were Irish farms still on good ground, numbering about 300. The Irish presence was still felt. They outnumbered the British by four to one in Cloghgenall, which belonged to Sir George Hamilton. The "British" had apparently disappeared entirely from the land at first granted to Sir George's brother, Sir Claud Hamilton.

The building programme at Strabane had a degree of success, but there were also signs of decay. In the town of Strabane itself success seemed assured, and the first earl put in lots of energy. He was also favoured by King James. A stone castle dominated the town of Strabane where there were about 100 houses. There was a mill, a bridge and a prison — not really a sign of civilisation. However, only too often the planters' houses and cabins were left uncompleted. Sometimes the colonies were left neglected. Sir George Hamilton lived in temporary quarters while work proceeded on his proposed residence in Derrywoon. The agent of the estates still had to live in a little thatched house on one corner of an uncompleted bawn. Pynnar had reported that the earl and Sir George were bound by a bond of £1,000 to carry out building on James Hay's original landed estates. The commissioners in 1622 found only the foundation of a castle which had been in the process of being built. It was a four-storey castle built on the land granted to Sir Claud Hamilton, and stood deserted and windowless. There was another bawn nearby which had not been touched for a number of years. Only at Strabane were the planters able to fulfil their obligations in relation to building. By 1622 the barony of Strabane had fallen into deep decline.

.   On the lands at Mountjoy there had been an important rise in the population since 1619. Pynnar reported that the land could support a considerable rise in the British population. He had reported that the area could raise 279 British men, which accounts for the number of approximately 140 families. Two versions of the survey agreed at the figure of 263 families from the precinct as a whole. Another school of thought places the number of planters at an estimate of 250 families. This does not imply that there were a large number of Scots settled in the area; only thirty or forty would appear to have been English. The number of Scots families, therefore, must have numbered between 210 and 220. The settlement at Mountjoy had shown a considerable amount of growth. There was little progress made with building. The only improvement since 1619 was the building of a bawn on Andrew Stewart's lands. There were still only three castles, and three out of the six bawns continued to be cemented with clay. Another one was built out of sods. In parts of Tyrone, not originally assigned lands, a few Scots reached the town of Dungannon. Only at Clogher had they established themselves to any extent. The certificates show that not only were practically all of Sir William's fifty-five tenants from Scotland, but so too were many of the tenants living on English territory. The certificates were open to exaggeration of the numbers of British present, and one can assume that the number of Scots settlers amounted to 120 families (in the barony). With those living at Dungannon and Omagh the total for the non-Scots areas of Tyrone must have amounted to 120 families.

At Armagh the names of the British population of the Fews were mostly Scottish, and no Scots resided outside the barony. By 1622 the Fews contained 220 British families, or about 440 men — almost double the number found by Pynnar. The Scots settlement had grown considerably since 1619, and Sir Archibald Acheson and John Hamilton were mostly responsible for this growth. All may not have been too well, as the statistics imply. Two of the freeholders we have seen returned to Scotland, one of them in 1620, and another coloniser moved to Clogher. An undertaker now threatened to leave the colony if his wishes were not taken into account. There was bound to be trouble in regard to the large number of tenants. But the colonisers sometimes expressed great dissatisfaction with the position on the land. There was a muster about 1630, but sources for this are hazy. We know nothing of why it was commissioned. It listed only fifty British men for Sir Archibald's and Henry Acheson's estates combined. This represented a decline of about 250 since 1622. Sir Archibald excelled in building. He had built stone houses together with bawns and outbuildings, and this competed with the best in Ulster. In other parts of the Fews there had been much progress. All the bawns in this barony contained clay as cement. Some of the bawns and castles needed to be demolished and rebuilt before they could act as a deterrent against the native Gaels of Ulster. The estate of John Hamilton, bought from Sir Claud Hamilton of Creichness, stood still without any fortifications. At Mountjoy success in planting British families had not been matched by the accompanying programme.

To assess the position of the Hamiltons in Cavan and Fermanagh it is necessary to take a closer look at the survey, and rely upon the final version of events, for neither certificates or drafts are available. The commissioners at Cavan and Fermanagh went to some pain to find out the true position in the counties and the number of British present. The commissioners reported the presence of forty houses inhabited by British families on one of the two proportions held by Lord Balfour in Knockninny. There were twelve fee farmers and leaseholders for one of the population, and five for the others. There were lands without landlords. Another estate contained forty British families. The British population in Cavan and Fermanagh in 1622 was quite small.

By 1622 there were some 102 British families (204 men) of Scots origin. On the lands owned by the Scots in Cavan there were 127 families (254 men). These estimates are close to Pynnar's count of 300 men and 282 men on the same proportions for Cavan and Fermanagh respectively. British families were now starting to decline in numbers. It is difficult to determine how many British tenants came from Scotland. The commission often remarked on the presence of English families, but they seldom made comments about individual estates. The survey does not distinguish between Scots and English settlers and the only reliable source is the 1630 muster roll. The number of Scots and English can be determined by the Scots and English settlers upon the land. The survey declared that a number of British on the land had come from Scotland. The survey only recorded about twenty per cent of the tenants being English. By this count the tenants remained on the one proportion remaining in Scots hands in Knockninny. The same is true of the estates in Clanee, County Cavan. In Magheraboy, County Fermanagh, about fifty to sixty families reported in the survey were of Scots origins. At Tullyhunco (Cavan) the British presence was more marked than elsewhere. This may have been a post-1612 development. The Hamilton family were the most successful and wealthy of the colonisers. After a death the land passed to Sir Claud Hamilton of Creichness's widow, who held it in trust for Claud's son, Francis. Between 1618 and 1622 Sir Claud's widow probably managed the estate. The position of the plantation had changed little from Pynnar's survey in 1622, but if the statistics of the muster can be trusted it increased a good deal between 1622 and 1630. New management had arrived and this may account for the large number of English on the estates in 1630.

Land was also obtained from the Scots by Englishmen. The Scots had received twenty-two proportions in Cavan and Fermanagh. By 1619 Englishmen had been substantial landowners, and the Scots were lagging behind. There were fifteen freeholders and leaseholders of English birth on Sir William Cole's land in Magheraboy. The undertenants identified as undertenants on British land went to the English in Fermanagh. By 1630 over ninety per cent of Sir Stephen's land had English tenants and English names. The Scots were discontented on the land and left soon afterwards. Some forty Scots lived in the area in 1622. In County Cavan only one of the original Scots estates had been purchased by an Englishman. In 1621 Sir Henry Pierce had bought Clandeboye and the estates from Sir James Hamilton. Almost immediately most of the tenants returned to County Down, so that they would remain tenants of Sir James. These were almost certainly Scotsmen. There is no indication that the twenty or so families who were colonising in 1622 were new arrivals, so we may assume that the Scots were now reviewing their position in Ulster.

The commissioners referred to immigrants as holding the best lands. The English commissioners favoured the non-Scots baronies, and regarded them as English. There was an overwhelming English presence and less than ten per cent can be classified as Scots. In Fermanagh there was a considerable body of Scots. However, by now the British families could be regarded as English. It seems reasonable to assume that about thirty or forty families originated in Scotland. A final conclusion regarding the Scots population in Cavan and Fermanagh must remain general. There were probably between seventy and ninety Scottish families on estates originally granted to Englishmen. There must have been in the region of between 220 and 240 families from Scotland living on these estates in 1622.

There was general trouble over the plantation in Ulster. No Scots were known to have noticed a considerable difference in the estates that they had originally settled. In numerous places the Gaels outnumbered the British. Lord Balfour had a large number of Irish tenants — seventy-four Irish families were found to be living on one of his proportions. Building of strong forts had begun, but they were left unfinished. The commissioners laid the responsibility for the poor showing on the shoulders of the landowners. There were exceptions to this position. William Baille had not as yet introduced settlers onto his lands. Baille's wife accompanied him and he toured his lands at regular intervals. They had built both a castle and a stone house; the usual bawns also went up. In County Fermanagh Gery Howe received a certificate in 1633 from his neighbours stating that he had authority over rented land. But the Scots were eventually settled on his lands. The commission told a different story in 1622, when it reported his absence in Scotland. His lands were mostly inhabited by Irishmen. His neighbours signed the certificate and a commission was sent to Fermanagh at the beginning of 1624; it was set up to find out how many Irish were residing on the lands. The general picture was one of apathy and neglect. For this King James blamed the landlords. Sir Archibald Acheson found himself displaced, even though he had land in Fermanagh. Sir John Howe was a landlord who normally lived in Scotland, and he lived under the ever-present threat of expulsion. They always found themselves in competition with the Gaels for land. The English would stay on a particular holding for a year only. Complaints were made that rents were too high, as on the estates of Sir James Craig. Sir John Dunbar had the habit of living off his Irish estates and he prided himself that he had good relations with his tenants and vice versa. Absenteeism tended to add to the political problems. The record of building in Cavan and Fermanagh was of a better nature than elsewhere in the escheated counties. However, the forts, castles and bawns were of little use without firm leadership to establish English rule in Ulster.

In Donegal the performance of the planters was little different to that in 1619, most notably in counties Cavan and Fermanagh. Portlough was the most fertile of the two regions originally granted to the Scots, who continued to settle — it was better settled perhaps than at Boylagh and Banagh. In Portlough the English population had not grown much since Pynnar's time. There were six estates in the precinct, and one can compare them with Pynnar's assessment. In Boylagh and Banagh there had probably been a drop in the English population. There had been little progress with building. Buildings, which the planters had established, had fallen into decay by 1622.

There is a third source for establishing the number of British settlements in Donegal. In 1625, or early 1626, Cornet Cartwright was commissioned to establish land in Donegal, probably with the threat of Spaniards at large. He sent letters to the bishops and undertakers in the county, requesting them to send in the names of tenants for whom they would be answerable. Few gave the names of the Irish tenants until he went to look for himself. He wrote to Falkland at the end of January 1626 and promised to send the list of the names he had collected, possibly for future use. The male population was divided into English, Scots and Irish categories. All these lists have not been found. Another one stated that Cartwright toured the planted areas. The 1622, 1626 and 1630 surveys were extremely complex and it would be unsafe to rely on Cartwright's abstract.

The 1620 muster is a comprehensive report in that it included all the baronies in County Donegal. One was omitted by the commissioners in 1622 and two others were excluded from a previous muster. Cartwright was gathering information on the British living on the lands belonging to the Anglican Church. The 1622 survey had only included the Church's tenants at Rathmullan, where Bishop Knox lived. Only those tenants in Raphoe were included in 1630. It is difficult to make out the plans of the planters and those who had power over them. Order had to be made out of confusion. This is the 1626 number of British in Inishowen on colonised land. The 1622 survey is perhaps the most reliable. There were therefore about 1,000-1,200 British males living on the lands granted them by laymen. It was not known how many were on Church land.

Under the new plantation scheme 10,000 acres were given to the Church in County Donegal. In 1632 Bishop Knox boasted that he had planted over 300 families of British Protestant settlers, the majority of which had come from Scotland. The families he introduced into Ulster could raise 500 men. About ninety to one hundred of these colonisers lived in Rathmullan. According to the 1630 muster, another 160 or so had received about 3,000 acres of land in the barony of Raphoe. The number in these areas and in Donegal (Protestant) were formidable. They were under Bishop Knox's control. It is probable that another twenty-five British men resided on Church land elsewhere in County Donegal. In all, including tenants on Church land, the final total for Donegal was 1,600. The Scots constituted a majority amongst the British, largely due to Bishop Knox's efforts in the poorer areas. English families were in the majority. The English-Scots ratio was in the process of becoming highly organised. It is certain that at the end of the reign of King James there were at least 1,060 Scottish males, of which about 500 were present in Donegal.

Cartwright's figures show just how precarious the English settlement was after thirteen years of colonisation. In all but one of the baronies the Irish outnumbered the British. In Donegal as a whole there were three Irishmen to every one Scots or English immigrant. The colonists would have to vastly increase their number if they were to establish a majority on the land. The same situation obtained throughout Ulster.

We now move to Londonderry. Here it is difficult to assess the number of planters, because the population in some of the surveys was not complete. In Londonderry about one third of the British were made up of Scots. The population of English to Scots probably changed little between 1622 and 1630. In 1622 the Scots must have numbered some 300 men; out of these 200 had settled on the land leased to Sir Robert McClelland from the Haberdashers and cloth workers.

A large number of McClelland's tenants may have entered Ulster after 1618. The male population of the Haberdashers rose from eighty to 123 during 1619-1622. The cloth workers increased from nil to eighty-six. The role of the English and the Scots in the early plantation period is not so tyrannical as is made out. When Pynnar visited Londonderry Sir Robert had only just leased the two Londonderry estates; also they had not yet leased tenants of the cloth workers' lands. The increase of the numbers of these estates represented the increase in interest in the Ulster lands. There were planters that had moved into the area before some preparatory work had begun. Sir Robert made a genuine effort to improve the situation. He outdid all other planters on the City lands. The circumstances under which he had to work were not easy, and his difficulties have been outlined in a previous chapter. There was a great increase in Scots into Ulster after 1618, but they were not of the same mettle as those in other counties. The British population had increased at Londonderry. It is certain that by 1618 there had been some immigration. Pynnar's survey showed only 432 males in Londonderry. However, his statistics for other lands were very often vague and it is hard to ascertain where increases were obtained. There is no evidence to show that the number of Scots at Londonderry was large.

There were the Church lands outside Donegal, and the bishops, as we shall see in another chapter, played a leading role. During King James's reign it is of interest that many Scots actually settled on the lands — vast tracts granted to the established Church in Ireland at the beginning of the colonisation/planting. The bishops were not obliged to introduce British tenants on the land of their sees. Bishops often leased out land to English and Scots gentry in blocks of 500 acres or more. There was, as a result of this, a division of responsibility. However, an absence of British tenants on Church lands did not mean that the bishop was not carrying out his responsibilities. A bishop could have a very important role to play in immigration, as witness the case in County Donegal. The sources had required that settlement on lay and ecclesiastical land be considered together. One bishop claimed that he had introduced a large number of planters. Knox's achievement was voluntary, and this makes it remarkable. The bishops were under no obligation to introduce British tenants. Every survey from 1611 did not take into account the bishops living on the estates. We must rely upon the muster of c.1630 to be sure of the sources. There were about 500 British men and women living upon Church lands outside Donegal on the escheated counties by 1630; about 180 of them came from Scotland.

The majority of British settlers lived in counties Fermanagh and Tyrone. Scottish names existed alongside the English names on the roll. No diocese in Ulster — with the exception of Raphoe — can be associated with just one county. The see of Armagh spanned Tyrone and Fermanagh, covering more land than any other see. George Montgomery, up to 1621, had been more energetic than the English bishops in inspiring work upon the plantation. At least fifty-eight of the British men who were contributing to the Church resided on land that belonged to the see of Armagh. The nationality of bishops was important, for the majority of the colonisers were Scots, who coveted lands in Ulster.

When the number of Scots is counted together, the total is some 3,200 Scotsmen out of between 6,000 and 7,000 adults. 4,500 Scots adults were estimated to be present when Pynnar made the survey. The latter total was regarded as a minimum, but it is reasonably sure that most of the Scots present in 1622 would have been counted. Nothing of any note happened in 1619 concerning the planters living on Church land, or estates owned by the English. The picture of events between 1619 and 1622 is gained by not looking at the totals of the two years but by contemporary totals for the Scots baronies or precincts. There was an overwhelming Scots presence in these estates, and a rise and decline in the number of British represents a movement of Scots.

Mountjoy and the Fews were originally granted to the Scots, and the British population had increased since 1619. At Strabane there was no change. In the four baronies in Cavan and Fermanagh the situation was one of decline. At Portlough, County Donegal, the planter population had increased to possibly twenty families. Within the Scots portion the net increase of some fifty British families since 1619 had taken place. It is certain that other incoming Scots families settled upon Ulster soil, but it is thought that the number was not large. The Scots increased at Londonderry and there was a general movement towards the city under Sir Robert McClelland — about another 50 families — and this has been pointed out.

The analysis shows that the number of planters settling in Ulster had declined, and at the end of King James's reign the situation was not satisfactory. However, the Scots records were better than the English. There were two Scots districts in County Tyrone — Strabane and Mountjoy — which contained some 550 British families. It may be compared with the 350 or so families in the baronies of Clogher and Omey. There was a decline in the British population between 1619 and 1622, whilst in the Scots areas it had simply failed to increase. 350 English families lived in the barony of Oneilland, compared with 220 Scots in the Fews. The 1609 survey shows all the planters holding 15,500 acres, in contrast with the humble 6,000 acres granted to the Scots. In terms of settlers the Scots surpassed the English. Only in counties Cavan and Fermanagh had the English done better than the Scots. By 1622 the English owned thirty-one proportions in Cavan and Fermanagh on which there were 440 British families. Fifteen lands were still owned by the Scots and there resided about half this number of British. Neither Scots nor English, however, could claim a majority and therefore domination in the plantation.

The Ulster plantation cannot be said to have been the worst in Ireland, despite the growing stagnation of the planters. The undertakers in Longford had done little and were likely to leave the country in a stagnant state. Only four out of the forty-eight undertakers in Leitrim were resident upon their lands. No building had been started, no leases had been issued, and the land did not seem to be like a plantation. The buildings of the planters at Wexford were praised, but it is difficult to ascertain the number of British that had settled upon Gaelic lands. Absenteeism was a problem, as elsewhere. The condition of the planters in the south of Ireland seems to have been the same as the position in Ulster. It might be thought that the progress of the plantation was better in counties Leix and Offaly, and that Munster would show more promise than Ulster. They had more time to become established. After the O'Neill rebellion of 1598 there was a long period of peace. However, the evidence is hazy when one compares the north with the south. Absenteeism was more a problem in Munster than in the north. Munster was made up of 240,000 profitable acres and it has been estimated that about 4,000 English males resided there in 1622. The Scots were granted 81,000 profitable acres in Ulster, upon which were planted about 2,200 Scottish men by 1622. This seems to prove that the Scots had to achieve a higher state of plantation than the English in the south. The English population in Munster was higher. Some men were counted several times since they were tenants of more than one landlord. Double counting occurred in Ulster but only occasionally, and it was usually spotted. It was impossible to count all the Gaelic lands, since a true number of settlers cannot be given. It seems that the English did better in the south than with the Scots in Ulster. The commissioners had sympathy with the position of the planters in Ulster. They too had to struggle with conflicting evidence under harsh conditions, for Ireland was a damp and rainy land. Efforts were made towards accuracy greater than that of previous surveys. Unlike previous surveyors they were not reporters. They were required to find facts and to make recommendations on what changes should take place.

On 19 November the commissioners issued a report which criticised the undertakers. The commission accused the landlords of making leases with no legal effect. They were able to expel leaseholders at will. They said that there was absenteeism and exorbitant rents. They reported that they could find no bona fide freeholders and that jury duties were expected from the already overburdened leaseholders — they were fined if they failed to serve. Most of the planters failed in their duties. They could not supply sufficient means to erect satisfactory buildings. The tendency towards large estates boded ill for the small landlord, and this was one of the reasons why the ordinary planters could not carry out their duties as landlords or tenants. Another section of the report dealt with reverence rather than with the performance of the undertakers. The importance of the estates was stressed, and with this King James was extremely pleased. It acted as a mainstay in this section and it was stressed that an early compromise should be reached with the colonisers. An agreement such as this would encourage settlement on the lands. The commission drew up a report of complaints about the behaviour of the undertakers. However, they adopted a positive attitude to those that their reports had criticised. As the undertakers had requested, the commissioners had recommended that the Gaels conforming to English culture should be allowed to settle on one quarter of each proportion. It seemed a good idea that the undertakers should allow Irishmen to reside on land set aside for them. If any land was allotted to Irishmen for more than twenty-one years the landlords were penalised. Concerning the former, it was recommended that a fine be imposed of ten shillings per family for each month the Gaels remained on the lands that were not set aside for them. In the case of the latter, forfeiture of the lands concerned was suggested.

Much money and effort was spent on the planters, not only in Ulster but throughout Ireland. It was put forward that a solution might materialise in about two years. If the recommendation had been implemented without delay it would have been well for all. King James seems to be more repentant about his generosity than concerned about putting the plantation back on its feet. It was said that the report put forward a true and accurate account of Irish colonial affairs. It was suggested that the undertakers be excluded from their lands and replaced with new settlers, who could be relied upon to carry out settlement and building in Ulster. As before, delay was the rule and not action, but no such extreme measures were implemented. For a year there was no activity, during which time the commissioners made themselves busy. By 12 December 1623 the English Council had not come to any decision. Even then it was only to order the Irish deputy to make sure that no Gael either left or entered the colonisers' estates. Another survey was initiated to discover how many Irish inhabited the various proportions and lands. These instructions were implemented in January and February of 1624. The British government vacillated and the undertakers submitted a second petition in July 1624; they pleaded that their original proposals be carried out. The document shows a unique account of the colonisers' point of view; it was not a reply to the various commissioners.

Under the leadership of Lord Balfour and Sir Archibald Acheson for the Scots, it was claimed that the failure of the undertakers to develop their property was due to the constant threat of forfeiture. This was a serious threat, and many sold their estates at the base rate. Rumours about the terms of forfeiture persisted, and British tenants became increasingly reluctant to lease their lands. It was said that there would be widespread prosperity for the planters. If help was to arrive then decay should have to be reported. As the Scots and English forsook their proportions, they had now an opportunity to recover their lost lands. The colonists became even more brazen than before, and they often settled on land without the owners' permission. There was a vicious circle. Re-entry of the Irish further stimulated the exodus of the Scots and English colonisers. Despite their shortcomings the undertakers fashioned some sort of civilisation in Ulster. Since King James expressed an interest in Ulster affairs, it was claimed the Ulster colony was prospering. The planters exhorted the king to send more colonisers to Ulster and to continue his interest in Irish affairs. Often the British imposed their means of building and planting on the lands. If such security was given then within a short period the plantation would flourish and be brought to perfection. The undertakers did not mention the true state of affairs in Ulster. The threat of confiscation would mean less effort and work upon the land. There was talk of not sticking to the agreements. The peak period of the sale of proportions was between 1613 and 1619. Colonisers continued to flock into Ulster. Those who sold their land to the fresh planters stood to make a considerable profit, considering that initially they had acquired the proportions free of charge. The presence of numerous tenants contributed to the statement that it was only impudence which made the Gaels put in a presence. However, the commissioners did not mention the charges of absenteeism and rack-renting.

There was much pleading, which brought about some extensive frustration. Many undertakers had established houses in the most inhospitable areas of Ulster. Their efforts had borne fruit. They had nearly managed to impose the English system of government in the province within a decade, when suddenly the whole project had been called into question and their achievement fell apart around them. There was a paralysis that gripped the English government since they had submitted their portion late in 1620. Three and a half years passed before anything was done to accede to the colonisers' requests. The undertakers were open to criticism and they were blamed for the loss of momentum suffered by the project. A second petition met with greater success than the first. The privy council had to deal with the matter immediately, and by 9 February 1625 action had taken place. The undertakers would receive double the amount of help for doubling their Crown rent. There was to be no forfeiture clause, and, subject to King James's approval, the Gaels who supplied the Anglican Church were given a handsome reward. A further concession took place six months later, whereby even nonconformists could settle on the land; but the matter did not end there. Negotiations between the undertakers and the government went on for another three years. The undertakers began to take out new patents by 1629. However, the agreements could be dishonoured if the planters and the Gaels fell out of line. Now a discussion took place concerned only about the nature of the plantation, and how the new policies should be implemented.

The principle of the revision of the plantation articles started to be considered coinciding with the death of King James. This marked the end of an era of Scots migration to Ulster. Between 1622 and 1625 the population of the escheated counties cannot have greatly increased. If there was a change the English government's delay in responding to the commissioners' report may have been likely to affect the decline and rise of the colonial situation. The Ulster Scots migration to Ulster does not stop here. Emigration into County Down did not stop when the settlements to the west had begun. Churchmen, as has been mentioned, played a leading role in the colonisation — they encouraged the Scots to settle upon Gaelic land. The performance of the chief landowners was praised as the tenants started to work on the land. It is a mystery why the Scots continued to settle in Ulster when the position on the land was precarious, and we have to delve deeply into Scots motives. There were economic reasons for the migration, and the trade which grew up between Ulster and Scotland has to be considered. Only by considering all the aspects — counties Antrim and Down, the Church, the undertakers and traders — can we obtain a true picture of the colonisation/plantation migration as a whole.

It is hard to ascertain the development of the Scottish settlement in Antrim and Down after 1610. Of all the various surveys only Carew's made any mention of this part of Ulster, and he does not go into detail like the earlier surveys. Population figures from Antrim and Down are derived from the unreliable musters or from casual remarks, which are not very trustworthy. The evidence is clear. It consists mainly of land grants and documents arising from myriads of disputes. Out of all the evidence Ulster emerges as the most important British colony in Ireland, so let us start by looking at the position of the Scots in County Antrim.

Chapter 10

The North-East Counties

In 1611 Carew discovered a large number of Scots living on the property of Sir Arthur Chichester at Belfast, Island Magee and on the lands of Sir Randal MacDonnell. The main residence of the Earl of Antrim was Dunluce Castle. The commissioners realised that this chief had built a strong fortification to keep out the Scots, English and Gaels. There were many lodgings and other rooms at Dunluce Castle. Dunluce had the status of being a town and had many tenants after the fashion of the Pale in the Dublin area. Other buildings of the MacDonnells were a large house at Glenarm and a "good castle" at Red Bay, both on the Antrim coast. The MacDonnells appear to have settled in County Antrim during the reign of King James I. The other lesser families were the Edmonstons and the Adairs. William Edmonston had originally travelled to Ulster with Sir Hugh Montgomery. He, along with his mother-in-law, obtained his denizenship in August 1607. He moved from County Down to County Antrim in 1609, where he bought 2,820 acres at Broadisland, in the barony of Belfast, about ten miles from the ancient town of Carrickfergus. Here he built two slated houses. The cost of settling a family was great, and the family fell into debt, so that in 1615 the family lands at Drantreath in Scotland had to be mortgaged for fifteen years. The Edmonston estates, however, in Antrim continued to flourish. William Edmonston died in 1626 and was succeeded by his son, who was able to raise, according to the 1630 muster, 151 British men, almost all of whom came from the Scottish Lowlands.

At Toome, William Adair had settled in the barony of Tyrone, and came from Wigtownshire. He was an important man in his own town, and was made justice of the peace in 1623. However, like other colonisers he was short of money. Sir Hugh Montgomery fell heir to some of the Wigtownshire lands. Adair had to face the authorities for debts he had acquired. It is not known when he went to Ulster. The first record of his presence is 1626, but some think that he arrived before that date. By 1620 his estates contained almost as many Scots as did Edmonston's. Ninety per cent of the men were Scots, according to a muster — 137 men arriving had been enlisted. Elsewhere in County Antrim there were scattered references to the Scots; names like Boyd, Shaw and Stephenson appear on the list for jury service, serving in Carrickfergus between 1613 and 1615. However, the MacDonnells of Antrim were the main landholders, and around the MacDonnells grew up a settlement.

The establishment of further MacDonnell lands was the fruit of the plantation in Ulster — the six escheated counties. There were nine townlands surrounding Coleraine and if there were improvements, the king would reduce the rent for the remainder by half. Sir Randal was rich and was much encouraged by this arrangement, and from then forward he flung himself into the running of the estates. The MacDonnells held one of the greatest buildings in Ireland, and he attempted to expand into Scotland, and this Scots adventure casts light upon how he managed his lands in County Antrim. Upon Angus MacDonnell's death Sir Randal leased most of his lands to his kinsman on the Isle of Islay. Soon after the lease had been obtained, the Islanders complained to the Scottish privy council concerning his administration. He had, he complained, spent four shillings (Scots) per day for every horse, cow or mare that grazed in the wastelands. He exacted twelve pence (Scots) for every sheep. Also he demanded forty-eight shillings (Scots) per annum from weavers and cordminders in Islay. The Islanders hated these impositions on the grounds that they were like the laws in Ireland. It is also certain that Sir Randal MacDonnell exacted similar dues in County Antrim. He was stopped from spreading his ambitions into Scotland. The Council issued an injunction against the application of *any foreyne or strange laws*. In the following year the Clan Campbell received grants of the island, and this put an end to Sir Randal's ambitions in Scotland.

Sir Randal still pursued his ambitions, and they were in general accord with the aims of the Crown. The Earl of Abercorn had much influence and had secured a parliamentary confirmation of his lands in Antrim. He matched his son to Abercorn's daughter and made the earl his son's guardian. The grant of lands were to be strengthened, and the king described Sir Randal as having great love, not only of the king but of the Ulster lands in general. In 1618 he was given recognition of his services as a coloniser, and the king created him Viscount of Dunluce. In 1620 he was created Earl of Antrim.

Between 1609 and 1616 Sir Randal granted land to some twenty-five Lowland Scots. The number of these transactions is not important. The nature of the leases is interesting. The contracts in the escheated counties were not as long lasting as the land agreements in Antrim. The shortest lease was for fifty-three years. More often they were for longer periods — for example 101 years, and one coloniser received a grant for 301 years.

The farms varied in size. There was one of only ten acres and another of 600 acres. However, other grants of land were for 150-300 acres.

John Shaw had obtained lands and had built Ballygally Castle in 1624. The size of the farms and the length of the tenures points to those receiving great opportunities, but as we have seen the process of plantation was slow, even though King James was proud of his creation. Such men would probably have drawn over other Scots after them. By 1641, a MacDonnell leaseholder was able to rent 375 acres to a yeoman. John Stirling rented another 347 acres to a "husbandman" named John Skeagh. George Alleyne's muster of 1618 was even more unreliable, for in counties Antrim and Down the landlords claimed that they were not obliged to muster except when the lord deputy at Dublin was himself present. Alleyne remarked that the plantation in the north-eastern counties was a model plantation not only to Ulster but to the whole of Ireland. Otherwise the only source of information is the 1630 muster.

The number of British males in County Antrim was uncertain and this was the situation at the death of King James. It was difficult to tell Scots from Englishmen. The muster showed that the MacDonnell lands contained most Scots. These were concentrated in two main areas — the barony of Dunluce, which included the fertile lands of the Route, or North Antrim, counted for over half of the British listed; and 268 colonisers were found in the Glenarm barony. By the end of the 17th century it was said that the hundred of this barony was populated mainly with Gaels. It must be assumed that the 268 lived either at Glenarm itself or along the Antrim Coast. However, the baronies of Kilconway and Curt between them could muster only 158 men.

Those who had settled on MacDonnell land seem to have crossed to Ulster in the 17th century, and names have survived from the Elizabethan age, but the majority of the colonisers of the colonies are associated with the Scots Lowlands. Great settlements were made and over half of the tenants of the English landlords came from Scotland, a much higher proportion than was common in the English-owned areas in the escheated counties. We cannot tell how many Scots were resident in Antrim. Over half of the tenants had English landlords, but by 1630 Antrim may have contributed between 2,000 and 3,000 Scottish adults. Antrim therefore provided adequate land for those who wanted to colonise the Gaelic lands.

The Scots settlement in County Down after 1610 continued to be dominated by Sir James Hamilton and Sir Hugh Montgomery. Hamilton had quickly become involved with the planters through his acquaintance with Lord Aubigny's estate in County Cavan. He put himself forward to be responsible for the two baronies he had helped. There was the possibility of a return from the freehold farmlands. The planters had second thoughts over whether to accept the offer or not. He only acquired a portion of the estate by way of a formidable lease. Even though there were large migrations to Ulster, Hamilton's claim to the land seemed unimportant. There is no reason to believe that he ever planned to settle the numerous Ulster lands. The colonisers had fallen into arrears in regard to rent, and by 1615 he had to divest himself of this part of his holdings. It could hardly be doubted that this retreat was the product of bitter land disputes in County Down. This undermined his position.

The first legal troubles in County Down broke out a little before 1610. By now Sir William Smith had laid claim to the Ards Peninsula. He claimed that it was part of his inheritance from Sir Thomas Smith, who had received it as a grant from Queen Elizabeth I. A tribunal was set up in 1622, which ruled that his ancestors had forfeited the right to the lands because of an inability to fulfil the settlement terms, but Sir William continued to press his claim. By 1623 both Hamilton and Montgomery were now defending their titles against Smith. The aim was to defend the two principal Scottish lands in Down, and their position was never seen to be in doubt because of the circumstances. By now a serious dispute had developed between the two Scots.

This was the Hamilton-Montgomery dispute and it often did little to help resolve matters. The Hamilton family's historian stated simply that Sir James had a lot of law suits with Montgomery about the land. The Earl of Abercorn was appointed as arbitrator in 1614, and his findings were not more illuminating. The dispute, Abercorn claimed, concerned the marshes of their land. We get an inkling of the nature of the dispute from the Montgomery manuscripts. It has been seen in the chapter on Antrim and Down that Montgomery had quickly begun to expand his holdings by purchasing part of Con O'Neill's estates. He had bought considerable timber and mining rights, as well as four townlands, from his Irish friend in 1606. At the beginning of 1621 he leased from O'Neill four townlands for thirty-three years. It is thought that more land had passed to Montgomery than this. He spent £1,000 on the Irishman's behalf by March 1612. He released Con O'Neill from a debt of another £1,000. Sir James Fullerton wrote to the lord deputy, saying that Con's estates should pass to James Hamilton's name alone. This meant that if Con wished to sell, he could sell only to Hamilton or otherwise only with Hamilton's permission.

In September 1612 the Earl of Abercorn arrived in County Down to arbitrate the dispute. It is unlikely that he was impartial for he was the cousin of Sir James and had reported adversely on Sir Hugh's attitudes in 1612. He handed down on 2 August 1615 lands favoured by Hamilton. By the terms of the settlements the two disputants were to sow the woods and lands acquired by Montgomery from O'Neill. In return Hamilton was to re-grant abbey lands belonging to Montgomery in 1605. It is not known why this last agreement was necessary, but it may well be that the boundary disputes concerning these lands. Montgomery regarded the decision as unfair. He pointed out, after it had been made, that it would mean that he would supply O'Neill at his own loss and to the advantage of others. The only concern troubling him was the confirmation of the lands originally conveyed to him by Hamilton. Because of his concern, he passed the case over to London, where in January 1616 he accused Abercorn of having regarded him as a charlatan. Sir Hugh managed to gain a re-grant from the Crown of all his lands to protect himself from the claims being made by Sir William Smith. He tried to argue that his re-grant involved Hamilton's claim as well as the claim of Smith. All was in vain. He had thought he could only obtain a postponement of the decision. By the end of the year King James consulted with the earl and recommended the implementation of the earl's solution.

Montgomery did not leave the matter here. Scottish planters were now complaining about all sorts of issues. He travelled to Holland to take up an issue. Hamilton may have won the first round, but Montgomery found it easy to copy the tactics of his enemy. Sir James could acquire property from him by examining the terms of the patents minutely. What would a close examination of Hamilton's patents reveal? So again Sir Hugh set out for Ulster to try to ruin his rival. None of the historians of the two families made any mention of Sir Hugh's movements or actions by 1617. He had written a letter on 15 November 1617 to owe money to John Wilkinson, recorder of Coleraine, and to Sir Hugh Clothsworthy, a large landowner in south Antrim. Wilkinson, now that there was trouble on the plantation, also travelled to London on criminal matters which he had against Sir James Hamilton. But he had no friends at court so that he had to ask Montgomery to help him through his connections.

The two men arrived at London some time after 1617, and Montgomery showed letters of patent, warrants and other documents to the attorney general, Henry Yelverton, a lawyer at Gray's Inn. The lawyers studied, and Sir Hugh obtained *their resolution under their hands, but the whole proceeding was erroneous*. The king had been foiled, and the patents were not valid in law. The letter did not explain why these patents were invalid or which of the patents were involved, but it did mention the king's letter to Thomas Ireland. In 1604 a merchant had been granted the right to acquire lands in Ireland, which would yield an income of up to £100 per year. Hamilton had arisen to become Ireland's assignee, with the lord deputy's approval. Montgomery revealed that the Crown had been misled by Hamilton's use of Thomas Ireland's letter. Montgomery remarked that he had undermined his own patent as well as those of Hamilton, the lord deputy and others. Montgomery had purchased lands from Hamilton, which had been acquired by Ireland's letter.

Montgomery's acquisitions did not end here. In 1611 word was spread abroad, and reached the English Council that the Bishop of Down and Connor and Dromore had tried to separate him from his wife. He had gathered information against the bishop. The Council was scandalised by the report and it demanded the bishop's immediate removal if the rumours were proven correct. Todd (the bishop) fled to Scotland before the authorities could act. After his escape it was discovered that he had embezzled most of the Church property under his control. Chichester made the accusation that Todd had tried to defraud some of the Scots gentlemen and others connected with the plantation. The deputy did not find any criminal fault committed by the Scots in dealing with Todd. So the matter rested there until 1617. Montgomery, having proved the invalidity of his enemy's position, proceeded to draw up articles establishing Hamilton as Todd's accomplice. The account of Wilkinson about Hamilton is ambiguous. At one instant it claimed that when confronted with the truth, Sir James would submit a promised restoration of the Church. However, Hamilton at the end of his letter maintained that he — Hamilton — should report and strive after the truth.

Montgomery's behaviour did not prevent the implementation of Abercorn's policies. This was put into effect in May 1618. By October 1618 Sir James Balfour had been sent over to investigate matters. Hamilton was ordered to show all the grants he had received during 1605-1610. All he could do was stall for time, by inquiring about the meaning of "exhibit" and other parts of the order. Hamilton, Abercorn's influential man at court, tried to soften the blow. The difficulty of Hamilton's predicament is indicated by the difficulty he had in complying with the order. Very little is known about these investigations. There was a casual remark in a letter dated 6 December 1618 saying that the marquess had just left Newmarket in a troubled state of mind.

For the next few years the records are silent on the case. On May 23 1621 the lord deputy, Viscount Grandison, wrote a long letter making complaints. One of his complaints was that many in Ireland might be subject to the investigation. The land scrutiny shows that the lands in Antrim and Down had been observed since the end of 1618 and the spring of 1621. The undertakers of the escheated lands were most suspicious of the deputy. The Hamilton-Montgomery dispute had contributed to the feeling of insecurity amongst the colonisers. This had hampered the Scots migration into most of Ulster.

Three English officials were in charge of the investigation along with the English Attorney General. The cases of eleven landowners in the area were affected. The committee issued its recommendation on 29 June, about a month after the lord deputy informed the king of the repercussions that the committee was having. There was such great complexity in the issues involved, that even the commons could not solve the problem. By the end of the reign of King James two more commissioners were appointed to disentangle the conflicting claims. The commons published its findings in June the following year. The committee was to examine the remaining claims in regard to the possession of property. The first issued its report on 8 December 1622, and the second on 22 June 1624. The two enemies, Hamilton and Montgomery, seem to have come to terms with their differences in 1626.

However, the truth about the Hamilton-Montgomery dispute may never be known. So many commissioners had been appointed that they found it very hard to understand the position in Ulster. No attempt had been made to sort out which lots of land were in question and which were not. What is important about the proceedings was the extent shown of the Scots holdings as indicated in a request made by December 1622. What is interesting is the way the dispute had arose. This reflects the very hazardous nature of the position. It has already been seen that what the Hamilton manuscript described as the *great expense in money and peace* was incurred by the bickering between landlords. The bickering goes some time back and explains Sir James's sale of his lease of the Trinity lands in 1615. He withdrew entirely from the escheated counties in 1621. He sold for £2,000 sterling the land that he had purchased from Lord Aubigny in County Cavan.

If Hamilton only had to pay some of the expenses for the battle with Montgomery, he might have been able to hang on to his Cavan estate. A conflict was also looming with the Crown out of the dispute with Montgomery. In 1621 the grants he had received through Wakeham's letter were still being investigated. He managed to stand up to the claim when both he and Montgomery were created viscounts. In 1623 or 1624 the moment of truth came. In the words of the family historian he was keen to conduct good relations with the king. He was on the point of ruination. Hamilton sold his lands in Cavan in 1621, which was a result of the troubles arising out of Montgomery's policies. Montgomery and Hamilton were the two principal Scottish colonisers in County Down. Charity was involved, but it was not the only casualty. The plantation at Down took place within the first eight years or so of its existence. This represented the peak of colonisation at this time in County Down. The Church entered the dispute and it was during this period that the greatest expansion of planter estates took place. Montgomery's success at plantation and the expanding of his estates, brought about a situation in which he fell out with his neighbours. Hamilton had not been backward about working his estates. He penetrated into the rest of Ulster, and his illegal acquisitions from the Church and the portion of land he took from Montgomery made one vast addition to his Down estates in 1610. In this year he leased in free-farm the barony of Dufferin from an Anglo-Irish family, the Whites. These estates were said to contain 15,000 acres of arable land, 1,000 acres of pasture, 10,000 acres of wood, and 2,000 acres of heath and moor.

Hamilton expanded further in 1616, when he leased eighteen townlands between Saintfield and Belfast Lough. Land was also leased to the O'Neills of Tyrone. Little was done from 1615 onwards. Hamilton made the purchase the year after the Earl of Abercorn had delivered the amount of the award in his favour. 1616 now seemed a good time for Sir James to further expand, but he was confronted by large threats. However, acquisition of land was not the only indication of success by a coloniser. The success of the two planters can also be judged by the numbers of settlers who were able to provide employment.

King James I praised the activities of Hamilton and Montgomery for their achievements in organising the land. Hamilton was made a viscount in 1614, was created an Irish privy counsellor and now commanded a horse and foot company. Most of the Scots who settled in County Down between 1603 and 1620 did so before the two principal Scots landlords fell out. The Montgomery manuscripts recorded that as early as 1610 Sir Hugh brought before King James a muster of 1,000 men. However, there is no evidence that a muster occurred during the early period. It was recommended that a special officer should be created, but nothing was done about it until 1618 by the Irish administration. Carew's survey came in 1619, the following year, but he did not make any comment about it having been such a large body of men.

Abercorn arrived in County Down on his mission to be a mediator in late 1614. He recorded that in County Down 2,000 well-armed men were ready to serve King James. This estimate took place when he was out hunting. There is also the evidence provided by the two elections held in the 1613-1615 parliament.

Three new towns arose — Bangor, Newtown and Killyleagh were incorporated before parliament was recalled, which would insure a Protestant majority. In all three the majority of the burgesses had Lowland Scots names. They would send favourable representations. The county electoral seats were closely contested. Hamilton and Montgomery were declared to have polled 130 votes as opposed to 101 for their adversaries. The election was disputed by the Irish. They claimed that some of those who had voted for the Ulster Scots were not freeholders. Also the Protestants could not gather as many as 100 bona fide votes. There was an examination of fourteen of Hamilton-Montgomery's supporters, all of whom were freeholders — so the sheriff declared the Scots to be elected. He dismissed the Irish claims as untrue and frivolous and not fit to be recorded in the report.

Neither of these accounts can be regarded as authentic, and there were probably negotiations on both sides. About 100 freeholders voted for the Scots, and it is possible to estimate the total population. The number of freeholders varied greatly from county to county, and precinct to precinct. In the well-established precincts (Strabane, Mountjoy and the Fews) it always ranged between ten and fifteen per cent. In County Down, following the Antrim example, new arrivals must have been in the order of between 1,000 and 2,000 families. It should be pointed out that some of those voting for Hamilton and Montgomery may have been of Irish extraction or plain

Norman-English. Not all of the newcomers came from Scotland. Both the successful candidates were Scots, and it is probable the majority voting for them were Scots as well.

The best settled lands in County Down were similar to the best settled lands of the escheated counties (Donegal, Londonderry, Fermanagh, Armagh, Cavan and Monaghan). However, the count of land being settled is unreliable. All of the counties present the same position. There were between 2,000 and 3,000 Scottish males in 1614. The two eastern counties in 1618 contained more British than some of the escheated counties. The muster of c.1630 supplies the only reliable evidence of the number of Scots living in County Down after 1614. If the figure for Island Magee in County Antrim can be excluded, the muster left Hamilton with 1,401 men and Montgomery with 1,317. About seventy-five to eighty per cent of these had Scots names. There may be some underestimation in the muster's figures, and the number of Scots living on these two men's estates had not grown by much since 1614.

There was, however, rapid development by 1614, but this was followed by a slower pace. This information we obtain from the number of buildings in the area. Carew visited County Down and found eighty newly built houses in Bangor, and twenty more at Holywood. The inhabitants of Bangor and Holywood were a mixture of Scots and English. Sir James had built a goodly stone house at Bangor, rising from the grounds of the ancient Bangor monastery in which lay a great stable and other houses. He planted orchards and fenced off the ground. Abercorn was impressed with the work that had taken place at Dufferin. His cousin also had built a castle at Killyleagh, the like of which could not be seen in the north. Sir James acquired his estates in 1610, and he wasted no time in starting construction work. His family history can be traced back to a Norman settlement in the region.

Thomas Raven had drawn up a map in 1625 of Hamilton's Down estates and this provides us with an interesting picture of the settlement at Killyleagh. At one end of the castle stood a tower, at the other end a corbelled turret with two gables set into the roof in between. A little town had grown up around the castle. It had four streets and contained seventy-five houses. Many of the houses had plots of land attached to them, which varied in size from three to thirty acres. Only a few of these houses were erected by Hamilton after he had obtained ownership of the barony. Before he purchased the settlement it contained ten castles, ten watermills and 1,000 gardens. Most of these proportions remained in the hands of the pre-1610 inhabitants. The 1630 muster listed only 366 British men in the barony, 119 in the towns, and 247 elsewhere.

Raven drew very erratic townland boundaries but seems to have exercised more care in the mapping of the towns. The other centres were not shown in as great detail as Killyleagh. Bangor is recorded as having seventy English-style houses, along with a number of small huts. Unless there are omissions from the map, the settlement and its population had not grown since Carew's time. Montgomery's town at Newtown contained 100 houses in 1611, all of Scots origin. He had also repaired the old Bangor Church, but he must have regarded this as a temporary residence, because when the Earl of Abercorn viewed the district, he found another house in the process of being built. Sir Hugh's other residence was at Donaghadee, a settlement of considerable size. In 1614 complaints had reached King James that there was a considerable traffic in stolen goods. It was decided to set up a ferry on which traffic should pass, and this was supposed to stop undesirables entering the area. An investigation was held to see if Donaghadee would make a good ferry terminus — Donaghadee could boast a large number of colonisers loyal to King James.

It took two years before Donaghadee was officially recognised at the ferry terminus to the British mainland — Portpatrick was chosen as the Scots harbour. The Scottish Council tried to set up a control system in 1616, but nothing was done on the Irish side. The Portpatrick-Donaghadee route became the main sea crossing between Scotland and Ulster. Even by the end of the 17th century this route remained the most popular. Donaghadee had become well established by 1614.

Most of the buildings had been erected by the time the Earl of Abercorn and his men had arrived in County Down — they had of course come from Scotland. Abercorn hoped to settle the Hamilton-Montgomery dispute. The dispute did not mean that there was a falling-off of immigration from the mainland. Until 1610 those Scots wishing to settle in Ulster had to put down roots in counties Down and Antrim; Down being more attractive. With the colonisation of the hinterland it became difficult to find new planters. Hamilton remarked about the competition between landlords to obtain settlers. He drew most of his tenants from Crown lands — not directly from Scotland, but from his Clandeboye estate. A considerable Scots settlement had taken place by 1614, thus easing the traffic between Scotland and Ireland. However, the settlement in Down did not decline after 1614. There is no evidence that Hamilton or Montgomery gave up hope in the same way as the planters in the main plantation. Hamilton studiously attended to his affairs according to an unsigned will in 1616. The will showed a great interest in continuing the plantation. There were several areas suitable for fishing and for other activities. In other areas the colonisers did not put pressure on the Gaels, and they were allowed to stay on their lands to the end of their lives, but without the right to pass on the property to their children. When they died, or broke the law, they were replaced by Scots *or other such tenants*. Hamilton does not seem to have treated the Irish with hatred. Nowhere else in his will did he abuse the Gaels of Ulster. The uprooting of the Gaels from their homes caused a lot of suffering, and Abercorn tried to soften this process.

There was considerable traffic between the Ards Peninsula and Scotland.

A commission was established to look into the Donaghadee ferry. It was estimated that it would take sixteen ships of from eight to ten tons each. No ships were permitted to sail until they had at least twenty shillings custom. The set fare for each passenger was eight pence. The minimum load for each ship must have been thirty persons, or the same in freight. Perhaps only seven or eight ships sailed each week. It was hoped that the ferry would bring much prosperity to the County Down coast and its hinterland.

Montgomery and Hamilton could raise 2,000 men within eight or nine years, but the interior of the county could only raise 400 planters after twelve years. The Ards Peninsula and Upper Clandeboye were fertile and free of mountains. Ruined old buildings provided material for the new settlements. In the escheated counties, neighbours' disputes often played havoc with the colonisation attempts. The dispute between Hamilton and Montgomery was bitter, but their efforts at colonisation did not crack under the strain.

The settlement at Down provided a calm beginning. Only six or seven years after the Scots had arrived, there was much peace and tranquillity in the region, so Down provided the best opportunity for immigrants. There were differences between the planters. The undertakers might fall behind their schedule and they feared for their position. Forfeiture must have loomed before Hamilton also. By the time this surfaced the plantation was well established. During the early years threats did not stop his efforts.

Hamilton and Montgomery had started to complain of stress, but their resources exceeded all those of the most wealthy colonisers in the rest of Ulster. By 1616 Hamilton had estimated that the lands alone brought him in £1,000 per annum. No similar figure has been recorded for Montgomery, but both men were insured for the sum of £100 towards the subsidy of 1615. The £100 equalled Abercorn's assessment and exceeded that of Lord Burley by £20 and that of Lord Ochiltree by £33 6s 8d. Subsidy estimated had no basis on income calculated in precise terms, but contemporaries had recorded Hamilton and Montgomery in Down as having equal influence and being on similar level to one of the richest of the chief undertakers. Hamilton had been able to weather the storm when it broke, and he lost very little. If he had been less able, he might have been foiled or dashed upon the rocks.

Hamilton and Montgomery had first made a name for themselves by promptly introducing settlers in large numbers. However, the usefulness for the planters did not stop there. After them came the Scottish landlords who established small estates in the same area. The two chief landlords persuaded their friends and relations to become freeholders. The process continued after 1610. Sir Robert McClelland leased three and a half townlands along the south bank of the River Lagan. One James Cathcart acquired some three or four townlands near Newtown, and a David

Anderson another near the same place. It is not known whether the smaller landlords attracted many Scots after them. The c.1630 muster did not mention them and possibly it embraced their tenants in the totals given for the land of the most important colonisers. McClelland sent an undated petition to King James, which indicates that at least one of the landlords intended to be Scots. The petition claimed that, after building a house on the land, he returned to Scotland to bring over to Ulster his friends, family and followers. In his absence some English occupied the land. Timber was sold and the house was broken into, leaving it in ruin.

The Scots bought land beyond the bounds of Upper Clandeboye and the Great Ards in County Down. One Alexander Julins obtained land in Kinalearty, south of the Upper Clandeboye. William Hamilton "junior" was busy and started residing at Downpatrick in 1616. A copy of the conveyance of the same year records that a certain Quintin Moore purchased a townland only two and a half miles from the same farm. Similar records of humbler Scots have been uncovered.

If one looks at the history of the Scots migration, more important than isolated purchases was the number of Scots tenant colonisers in non-Scottish areas. In 1610-1616 an inquiry revealed that the Scots had leased the land in the Little Ards from Rowland Savage, a descendant of a Norman family which had settled in the area. The Scots were now widespread in County Down. Englishmen also held lands, and those belonging to the Church contained 950 men by 1630. The names on the rolls suggest that just over half of the colonisers had come from Scotland. Down contained somewhere between 2,500 and 3,000 Scottish males. This meant that counties Antrim and Down could raise between them 4,000-5,000 male Scots. There was in the region of two male adults to a family, so the two counties contained more Scots families than all the escheated areas put together.

Of the two north-eastern counties the activities in County Down seem to be the most interesting. The colonisation of Down seems to have been more successful than that of any other of the Gaelic lands. The character of the plantation was of paramount importance. Difficulties could not be avoided. Boundary laws were set up, and all this happened without detailed knowledge of the country. Surveyors' methods were imperfect; there was a total absence of enclosure. To survey such hostile conditions, a man had to possess boundless energy, drive and ambition. Despite superior conditions in Down, illegal deeds often took place.

Chapter 11

Presbyterians

During Elizabeth's reign the Church had been the stumbling block in her attempt to bind Ireland to England. Elizabeth had failed to convert the Gaels to Protestantism. The Irish did not take to the faith of the foreigner, partly because the new doctrines were not preached in the Irish language. Also the Pope proclaimed that the Irish clergy were devout in Ulster. England's political weakness in Ulster made the imposition of conformity impossible. The English Church therefore was despised and ignored by the Irish and neglected by its sponsor. Only a year after James ascended the throne, Sir John Davies wrote that the churches were ruined and fallen to the ground. There was no divine service, no christening of children, no receiving of the sacrament, no Christian meeting or assembly.

The Anglican Church achieved very little in the face of this adversity. England had not yet lost the ideological battle. It regarded Ireland/Ulster more as a religious vacuum than a Catholic stronghold. Sir John compared the priests in Monaghan with those in England during Mary's reign, and said that the Gaels might be easily converted. William Lithgow, a Scot, reached the same conclusion after touring Ireland in 1619. He remarked that Ulster's clinging to Rome was caused by conservatism rather than conviction. He found that priests and laity had very little knowledge or belief in Christianity. They were ignorant of the mission of Jesus. Many Gaels feared the power that the British had over them. Another Scot, Robert Blair, arrived in Ulster at the end of King James's reign, to find that the Irish priests were generally ignorant people and suffering from drunkenness.

All of this was Protestant opinion and can be compared with the Roman Catholic assessment of about 1614 that recorded nearly all the Gaels were of the Roman Catholic Church. It was perhaps a delicate allegiance in a turbulent age. It would have been surprising if religious knowledge had permeated deeply through the population. Roman Catholicism survived the assault of Elizabeth and company. That Roman Catholicism survived was due to the weakness of the established Anglican Church. It is possible that had the Anglicans used Irishmen to teach Irishmen in Irish, then it might have made a number of converts. It was claimed that Catholic priests were leaving the Anglican Church. Lord Deputy Chichester and the Irish Council reported in 1605 that they could not find a priest in Armagh willing to celebrate mass in accordance with King James's laws. The use of the word "law" is of note. Catholic priests had no hesitation in breaking the English laws, for no Gael had respect for them. On the other hand it was proclaimed by the Bishop of Derry in 1611 that he had admonished the renegade priests, and he told them not to preach the Catholic faith in conformity with that of Rome in her more moral moments. He managed to convert three priests in his diocese and continued to uphold the faith of the Church of England. It is true to say that the Gaels and the Anglo-Irish nobles held fast to Rome. The bishop's experience in the north led him to believe that the Anglican Church had to make considerable headway amongst the Gaels and their Gaelic Church.

King James had some misgivings about the situation in Ulster. At the start of his reign the Venetian ambassador reported the government's intention to send enthusiastic priests to the Emerald Isle. A year after the main plantation had begun, the lord deputy, Chichester, wanted to use persuasion as far as the Gaels were concerned and not try to impose the Oath of Supremacy and Allegiance, except on office holders. On the whole the Anglican Church adhered to its established ways. In 1619 a lot of contempt for the Protestant pastors was voiced by their Roman counterparts. Most parishioners were uneducated and some ex-soldiers became pastors. The 1622 commission found that for 2,492 parishes there were only 380 preachers or ministers. On these figures the position and success of the plantation and colonisation of Ulster took place.

With the accession of King James in 1603, Protestantism in Ulster was a failure. The majority of the sees had no Protestant bishop, with the possible exception of Down, where there were some English. The reformed faith was confined to the garrisons. The 1622 visitation of Ulster revealed that there were still many shortcomings both in building and in personnel. Protestantism, having failed to convert the Gaels, meant that the colonisers remained largely a British veneer. But it cannot be denied that Protestantism had made some headway in the twenty-two years of King James's reign. The Anglicans started from virtually nothing, but they soon held a powerful presence in Ulster and in some parts were a living force.

Part of this success was due to the position of the Protestant planters, but they needed leadership. It is wrong to suppose that the Anglicans failed to produce effective Church leaders. Brutus Babbington, the Bishop of Londonderry, said that he had converted a number of priests in his diocese. He was an Englishman. It is true to say that it was the Scots who provided leadership and effective colonisation in Ulster.

Few Englishmen could speak Irish; in early 1576 it had been proposed that Gaelic speaking Scots should be brought to Ulster to preach the gospel. However, this proposal did not work whilst Queen Elizabeth was alive. One Scot, Denis Campbell, became Bishop of Limerick during her reign. Sir John Davies repeated the suggestion and it may be due to this that Campbell was raised to the three sees of Londonderry, Raphoe and Clogher later that year, but Campbell died before he could take up his duties. King James now appointed George Montgomery Dean of Norwich and the king's chaplain. Montgomery knew little or no Latin, unlike Campbell. As we have seen, Montgomery played a great part in bringing settlers to Ulster. His efforts at claiming land for the Church are worthy. He was successful in sustaining their efforts. For much of the year the new bishop was an absentee, living in England. This was frowned upon by Davies, who regarded a delay as a forsaking of duty. However, Montgomery put most of his time to good account, pressing the Anglican Church's right to land. Chichester used the bishops as an intermediary at court to plead the expansion of Trinity College's endowment.

A little before 1607, Montgomery made a survey of the sees over which he had authority. There was much reaction from the many little churches. All had Gaelic names, but some were of Scots origin, i.e. McReady, MacCawell, McTaggart and MacM'Collagan. Some were able to speak Scottish and one had a son studying in Glasgow. Most of the planters were nominal Roman Catholics. Montgomery went to England where he licensed nineteen preachers to serve in Ulster. Still present in 1619 were James Heygate and Edmund Hutton. Heygate, who had been an archdeacon of Clogher, was a Scot, becoming a denizen in May 1617. Hutton sounds like an English name, but the remaining seventeen must have come from Scotland.

It took the English two years in which to arrange matters within the plantation, and George Montgomery worked very hard in the interest of his Church. He persistently made claims for land which had formerly belonged to O'Neill of Tyrone. When faced with a jury which decided claims he then tried to influence it into changing its mind. He was assured by King James that the plantation would be strong in Ulster. In the face of opposition from the administration at Dublin he won his case and also had a little praise for some of his opponents. The Church was originally proposed to receive 75,000 acres. Now it received an amount just short of 100,000 acres. At this point Montgomery was transferred to the see of Meath, although he still remained Bishop of Clogher. He was not at all divorced from Ulster affairs and busied himself with the Church of Ireland, the state Church in the island. He was not only concerned with the state affairs in Ulster. The vacancy he left was to another Scot, Andrew Knox, Bishop of the Isles, who was appointed to the bishopric of Raphoe. Knox had proved himself to be well qualified to become a bishop in Ulster. He graduated from Glasgow University in 1579, and for a while was minister at Paisley until he became Bishop of the Isles. He led an armed expedition to the Isles, and imposed upon the chieftains the Statutes of Icolmkill, which meant churches were to be repaired and vagabonds chased from the Isles. All the gentry were bound to send their eldest sons to the Lowlands for education. Knox witnessed the building of churches in places where no churches had existed before, and provided the clergy with stipends to serve the parishes.

After his appointment to the diocese of Raphoe in the summer of 1610, Knox set himself the task of reforming the Established Church with the same energy Montgomery had shown in providing for its endowment. Within a year of his appointment, and after visiting Ireland, he had gone to court to press for the adoption of eleven articles designed to outlaw Roman Catholicism from Ireland and place Protestants in the offices. Archbishops and bishops he said, should hold a convention to uncover which priests had been deposed and which ministers were to pass through the country preaching the word, trying to convert the country to Protestantism. Those who did not conform were to be excommunicated. Their names were to be forwarded to the lord deputy so that punishment could be meted out. He ordered that the bishops should have to be resident and that consideration should be given to the establishment if any one refused to acknowledge the Anglican Church.

Knox had considerable success in the Isles, but he did not understand the situation in Ulster. Scots ministers were expected to travel the territory making conversions to Presbyterianism. However, it would take more than argument to persuade the Established Church to change its attitude towards dissenters. His efforts at complaining were not very good. Knox failed to understand and he was for excommunication if Catholics did not worship in the Church of Ireland. In July he travelled north to his Scottish diocese, and after this set foot upon Ireland, reaching Dublin. It was an eye-opener on the real state of affairs in the north. To bring about change seemed impossible. In a letter to the Archbishop of Canterbury, he said that *in the Kingdom and the harvest of the land there was to be labourers*. He wanted to make all of Ulster Protestant. In the next year Knox was still enthusiastically submitting suggestions for reforming Ireland. In 1612 he had given up the task of establishing the Reformation in Ulster. His own diocese would have been against the Roman Catholic Church. He had introduced into the Irish parliament a further series of proposals, introducing a bill in the 1613-1616 parliament requiring the Irish laity to attend Protestant services. But Knox's idea had little support. From now on he was to concern himself to bring that part of Ireland directly under his control.

As far as bishops were concerned there was no obligation to plant with British tenants — a rule introduced in October 1612. There was no question of compulsory British settlement. However, Knox proceeded to colonise his lands immediately after his appointment. The revenue from Raphoe (amounting to only £30 per annum) was sufficient to support a bishop. There was also the matter of additional charges that the importation of settlers would incur. King James provided Knox with an additional annuity of £100 as well as his normal stipend. Tenants were reluctant to go to Donegal. It was only with great difficulty that he managed to persuade some of the Scots to emigrate. On their arrival he persuaded some to accept favourable terms. There was a crisis in the land market. The Scottish were at first reluctant to come; a feature of the leases granted to planters upon their arrival was that he had to grant more favourable terms if there was not to be a decline in the market. The bishop never provided a satisfactory enticement for the Scots to come over to Ulster. Some overcame their doubts and reluctance to colonise in the north of Ireland. It came about that Bishop Knox had released his leaseholders from their obligations to pay rent during a war or a rebellion. This reflected the attitude of the colonisers who wanted to establish a firm position for Protestants in Ulster. Knox tried to appeal to the government to station twenty-five soldiers near his home. There was an overall atmosphere of uncertainty.

The Gaels hated the colonisers, and Knox's achievement may have appeared the more remarkable. In 1619 he received a grant of up to 300 denizenships, as has been stated in a previous chapter. He claimed that he had settled financial matters with the Protestant families. From the original £30 per annum in 1610, the annual profit of the plantation had risen to £200 by 1616, and by 1629 to £650. However, the bishop's estimate in 1632 fell short of the official figure of 1629. Such improvements rivalled that of even the best lay planters.

Knox went about his secular task with great enthusiasm, and he also did not neglect his spiritual vocation. The lord deputy had great praise for Knox, claiming that he had done much for the Church at Raphoe. By the beginning of 1612 many members had crossed to Scotland to preach to a large number of parishes. After two years had passed, the Gaels had reached the situation whereby all priests had a parish.

There was much Protestant success. Fifteen ministers were listed, including the dean, twelve of whom had probably come from Scotland. All but one of the colonisers had university degrees. In only seven cases one minister looked after a single parish. Two parishes shared a minister, whilst two ministers served three parishes, and one was in charge of five small parishes. When a minister had to be looked after, he had at least a ready minister, cleric or curate to help him. Raphoe was a large diocese, judged against other plantations. Knox drew from Scotland some of his colonisers, three of whom could speak Irish. As a consequence he employed a number of Irishmen. The schoolmaster at Donegal was converted to Roman Catholicism. At least half of the fourteen ready ministers were Irish, three of whom were ex-priests.

The success of the Church in Donegal cannot be ascribed to unusually favourable conditions. Most of the land that the planters tried to sow was moorland. It was difficult to collect the rent because the Gaels practised a form of colonisation. As late as 1622 a parish valued at £32 a year was obliged to support a minister, a curate and an Irish leader. The curate received £10 per annum, which must have come out of the general funds. One of the grievances of the clergy concerned the practice of supporting more than one minister for each parish. The Scottish leader received a yearly stipend of £3. The situation differed from parish to parish and these figures do not represent extremes, but come close to the typical.

The parishes had slim resources and had to pay for the repair of churches as well as financing the clergy. In 1610 the diocese had a few churches with roofs, whilst a newly arrived minister who came across a house in which he could live must have considered himself very lucky. In Ulster even a bishop had to live in a thatched cabin. The 1622 visitation found that half of the churches in Raphoe were in a serviceable condition, and many ministers had built houses. Sometimes a local undertaker and his tenants helped towards building costs. The visitation cited one such case. The clergy complained that building was a great expense. This showed that they incurred most of the burden. Much remained to be done by 1622; there were enormous problems to be solved in Bishop Knox's diocese, down from himself to the lowliest clerk. The people, however, acquitted themselves well.

Only one other bishop in Ulster in the escheated counties originated from Scotland, and this was the Bishop of Clogher. Knox's diocese covered most of Fermanagh and parts of Tyrone and Monaghan. We have seen that George Montgomery retained Clogher when transferred to Meath. Montgomery died in 1620 and was succeeded at Clogher by Dr James Spottiswood, brother of John Spottiswood, Archbishop of St Andrews. He had graduated with an MA from Glasgow University in 1583, having been born in Edinburgh. In 1567 he entered upon first the king's service and later the queen's. He was to accomplish great things; in 1603 he was ordained and preferred to the rectory of Wells in Norfolk. In the same year he left the royal service, until, in 1616, James sent him to reform St Andrews University. After this he returned to England and happened to be at Court when news of Montgomery's death broke. He applied for the vacant see at Clogher, and he was accepted. He crossed to Dublin in April 1621, three months after his appointment. He remained at Dublin for a year, before making his way to Clogher.

The poor conditions at Clogher must have shocked him and prompted him into reform. His predecessor had been a great supporter of the Church of Ireland before the plantation. However, after 1610 the see of Clogher did not match up to Bishop Knox's performance in Donegal. By 1622 about half the incumbents in County Tyrone and Fermanagh were ruined or inconveniently situated. The absence of clergy was a serious problem, as well as the poor condition of the buildings. The undertakers were trying to deprive the Church of its endowment. Spottiswood's immediate task was to restore the lands which had been usurped. Here he ran into serious difficulties. For example, Sir John Wishart of Pittaro had refused to pay the rent for twenty-four townlands he had leased from Knox. Sir James Balfour (to be Lord Balfour), liked the idea of any school land worth £240 a year. The lands lay adjacent to his own, but there was much bribery afoot which had to be dealt with if the plantation could be restored.

There was a great atmosphere of hatred and a feeling that the performance of the Anglican Church in the diocese could in no way compare with that of Raphoe. There were six ministers in the diocese who had crossed from Scotland: three did not reside in their parishes, and of the three that did, one combined clerical duties with being an undertaker. The record of settlement was poor. Church lands at Fermanagh contained more than 100 British males, according to the muster of c.1630. Montgomery was held responsible for the poor showing, not Spottiswood. Here it is evident that the leadership factor, which was often needed in the lay plantations, played no less a role in determining the success of the Anglicans in given areas. Bishop Knox was a star performer for the Church, and he had never been influenced by the atmosphere of England.

In counties Antrim and Down, King James appointed two Scots successively to be Bishop of Down and Connor. James Dundas accompanied Knox to Dublin in 1611. They could help him argue the case for the reformation of the Irish Church. Knox was so pleased with Dundas that he persuaded him that he should receive a permanent appointment. Little could be done immediately to find him a post. Todd resigned the two sees of Down and Connor, and Dromore, and with the help of John Spottiswood (the Archbishop of Glasgow) proposed four Scots to take Todd's place. It is certain that one of these was Dundas. Lord Deputy Chichester approved Knox's nomination. The deputy had learnt to dread the arrival of the Scots bishops in Ireland, for he found them very quarrelsome. He had reason to fear such an appointment, as the diocese lay in that part of the country in which he was supposed to reside. He did not like the idea of ending his days surrounded by turbulent Scots, who more than likely would stir up trouble. The Council approved the lord deputy's appointment and Dundas became Bishop of Down and Connor early in 1612. Tragedy loomed — soon after taking up the appointment he died.

Now the Scots living in the diocese persuaded Robert Maxwell, Dean of Armagh, to put himself forward as their new bishop. The Dean of Down was a competitor as well. Chichester recommended the Bishop elect of Dromore, John Tanner. None of these, in the end, received the appointment.

On 29 November 1612 King James wrote to Chichester informing him that one Robert Echlin, born in 1576 and a graduate of St Andrews University twenty years later, should become minister at Inverness in Fife. Little is known about him so the reasons for his selection remain obscure. Maybe, like Dundas, he owed preferment to the Bishop of Raphoe. Echlin and the Dean of Raphoe had graduated from St Andrews on the same day. Knox may have had first-hand information about Echlin. He may well have had influence on who the next bishop should be in view of the sudden death of his previous nominee.

He arrived in his diocese in 1613, but Echlin's greatest problem was the desperate financial position. His predecessor had to rely upon the good nature of King James, and also the Archbishop of Canterbury, as a result of Todd's misrule. Even though Dundas had a short tenure, the Anglican Church lost most of its assets. Montgomery and Hamilton between them had leased twelve townlands from Dundas. The dean and chapter gave these proceedings their assent, but, by the time of Echlin's arrival, the copies of the lease had been lost, so he could not prove the Church's ownership. Montgomery and Hamilton now proceeded not to pay the rent and claimed the land as their own by right of being in possession. Many knew that the land belonged to the Church. Also Montgomery refused to pay rent to the Anglicans for land that he leased from them. They said that the borders lacked clear definitions.

There was considerable maladministration and a great appetite for land as the planters carried on their duties. They had so impoverished the diocese that it could only yield £50 in one year. Echlin travelled to London in order to complain about the situation in Ulster to King James. The king now appointed a freeman to look into the affairs and to enforce those colonisers who had obtained Church land by fraud to restore these lands to the Church. George Montgomery was one of the members of the commission. He was a great supporter of the Anglicans. Now Montgomery was appointed to a neglected diocese along with Spottiswood. Echlin did not suffer as badly as Montgomery. The two men were able to show that the progress of the Protestants in Ulster was well under way.

It is difficult to assess the number of Scots that went over to Ulster during King James's reign. In the escheated counties not all the Scots ministers who had settled did so at the behest of bishops. However, it is certain that Montgomery and Knox were responsible for the arrival of many colonisers. In counties Antrim and Down the bishops had less control over the selection of incumbents than in Clogher and Raphoe. The condition of churches in Down and Connor in 1620 was worse than anywhere else in Ulster. Out of 150 churches, only sixteen were in any great state of repair, whilst in other cases the original buildings had disappeared. There were forty-three resident ministers of whom fifteen or twenty were Scots. It has been estimated that about ten Scots had graduated from Glasgow University in Scotland. There was the appointment of Echlin and he was appointed as a graduate who was not a St Andrews man. It is often a problem to find out how much of the plantation was due to Echlin's influence. All Church lands in counties Antrim and Down were omitted in the c.1630 muster. In County Down the population on the colonised land was incorporated with some other estates. The Scots bishops had performed well. It had been Montgomery that had voiced that he wished some land of the Church. Spottiswood and Echlin had tried to swiftly restore their sees lost through neglect or the dishonesty of their predecessors. Bishop Knox had shown just how effective a bishop could be in promoting the cause of Protestantism when resolution was applied.

The Scots bishops therefore played a great role in the Ulster colonisation — mention has been made of the great number of ministers who left the mainland to take up appointments. Statistics about these clerics are hard to find. It is difficult to trace the origins of those with names such as Richardson, and a few of those who came under the 1622 visitation were noted for being non-resident. Some had land in Ulster and may not have taken up residence in the province. Sometimes they did not stay in the plantation. Scots clergymen migrated to Ulster during the reign of King James, this being apart from bishops, and there were many others who may have come from Scotland. Many Scots may have migrated to Ulster on the initiative of the bishops. Sixty-four bishops' nationalities are known. Forty-nine held livings in bishoprics; forty held livings in bishoprics occupied by Scots. There was mention of the presence in Raphoe of ministers named by Knox, and there was little doubt about who was responsible for their presence. In Echlin's diocese Hamilton possessed six presentations; Montgomery "two or three"; Sir Randal MacDonnell of the Glens of Antrim had several. Lord Ochiltree had brought over a minister with him in 1611. Both Douglas and the Duke of Lennox possessed rights of presentation. So County Down was not the only diocese where a major landowner exerted influence on the migration and colonies made by the Scots clergy.

It was also possible to obtain land in Ulster by directly approaching King James. The Crown had a few livings ready for appointment. In addition to the bishoprics, James had the right to nominate all deaneries in Ulster as well as archdeacons and canonries. John Gibson, a Scot, and Dean of Down, owed his appointment to King James as did Robert Maxwell, Dean of Armagh. Maxwell had been a minister in Ireland for many years before becoming a dean. In one case the Archbishop of Armagh was told to find an ecclesiastical position for one James Stewart who was without any post for a year. However, there is no evidence that Stewart ever settled in Ulster.

Only after the parliamentary ratification of the Articles of Perth in 1621 did the colonisers have an attack of conscience. After 1621 the only minister to travel to Ulster had been Robert Blair, who arrived in 1623. Blair had been appointed regent at Glasgow University in 1616. He publicly opposed the Perth Anglicans at every opportunity and he soon fell into disfavour with Archbishop Spottiswood and the principal of the new university, James Cameron. As a result of the controversy he had to resign from his position as regent, but it is unlikely that he would have settled in Ulster. Viscount Clandeboye had invited him to succeed the ageing John Gibson as minister of Bangor.

Two Scots clergymen were banished to Ireland on account of their religious beliefs in 1625 — they were John Dunbar, minister at Ayr, and Richard Dickson, minister of St Cuthbert's, Edinburgh. Neither left for Ulster in King James's reign. There is no evidence to show that Dickson ever reached Ireland, and Dunbar's sentence was postponed until after James's death. This prompted many Presbyterians to take up residence in Ulster.

Persistence may have prompted many Scots to go to Ulster — it was a tiny New World, where the planter rowed up and down the River Bann and other waters. Most of those that did cross held Calvinist opinions. Blair was against going to Ulster and he believed that religion had suffered at the hands of both laity and clergy. When he eventually arrived, Blair discovered many men who would sympathise with his opinion. Many Scots in Ulster only half-heartedly believed in the system and beliefs of the Churches (Anglicans, Calvinists and Presbyterians). Echlin encouraged Blair and his associates, but in the reign of Charles I he had turned against them. Bishop Knox, at Raphoe, continued to the end of his life to allow candidates to worship in accordance with conscience. Calvinism was not only associated with the Scots clergy for, as early as 1621, the Archbishop of Armagh remarked that Sir Hugh Montgomery, Viscount Clandeboye, allowed ministers that had suffered persecution during King Charles's reign to take up refuge in his house. He also invited Blair and others of similar opinions to work as ministers on his estates.

It is thought that Blair exaggerated when he said that before his arrival little had taken place to establish religion in Ulster. He did not give any credit to Bishop Knox and Echlin, who had achieved much in their early years of colonisation in Ulster. Blair was writing after 1636, after the religious revival in counties Antrim and Down, which started soon after the death of King James I. It could be said that religion was in a poor state until the arrival of Blair upon the scene. This information was obtained by an Englishman and the author only dared to sign his name with the solitary initial R. He was probably John Ridge, minister at Antrim, and he declared himself to be a clergyman in the north of Ireland. He was surrounded by colleagues who were mostly from Scotland. The Scots ministers he described as being mean and for walking the streets. He could not find them determined about any more than the taking up of their vocations. As a result of the new blood many sorts of people came from afar — as far away as twenty miles — to the present congregation of between 700 and 1,500 souls. This enthusiasm must have been unique in Ireland.

The colonisers' leaders, particularly Blair, had now made a permanent mark upon Ulster soil and on the ordinary people in their parishes. Nationally the influx of the Scots clergymen had been expressed in the Calvinist nature of the 104 articles passed by the Church of Ireland, but only Knox can be regarded as holding strong Calvinist views. In actual fact, the articles were English in origin, not Scottish Calvinist. The articles eventually incorporated nine Lambeth articles of 1595 which Queen Elizabeth I had rejected. The influence of the Scots on the nature of the Irish lands was negligible; the adoption of the articles provided the Scots with a suitable environment in which to work. Persecution of the Scots in Ulster began in the reign of King Charles I, but the roots of Scots Calvinism were too firmly rooted.

The Scots had made a great contribution to the Protestant cause in Ireland. If we look at the history of the plantation in Ulster, the purpose was to convert Roman Catholics to Protestantism. Sir George Hamilton of Greelaw, like his father, Lord Claud Hamilton, was of the Church of Rome. The situation had arisen to be one of the most anomalous circumstances in the entire period of colonisation/plantation. His brother died leaving only minors. Sir George eventually controlled five of the proportions at Strabane. As a result of Sir George's influence, both Abercorn's and Sir Claud Hamilton of Schawfield's children were converted to Roman Catholicism. The anomaly arose that one of the most successful parts of the Scots plantation in the escheated counties was led by Roman Catholics. The authorities as early as 1614 knew about Sir George's religious beliefs. Instructions were given that he should be forced to conform or be expelled from Ulster, but the instructions were ignored. Sir George lived on in Ulster and retained his faith. In 1622 accusations of discrimination were made against Protestant settlers in the barony of Strabane and Sir George was accused of surrounding himself with men of his own religion. With the accession of King Charles to the throne, Sir George and the young Earl of Abercorn continued to bring Roman Catholics to Ulster from Scotland, amongst them some Jesuit priests. The bishop admonished that unless the movement was stopped, rebellion would break out at Strabane. As a result of official incompetence and a series of family deaths in the Hamilton family, Sir George Carew had been able to introduce Roman Catholics into the heart of Ulster.

It is safe to assume that most of the colonisers were nominally Protestant. They do not seem to embrace strong religious opinions. There is no evidence during James II's reign that there were overwhelming reasons why the Scots and other Protestants should leave Ulster. The religious complexion of the province was the result of the leadership provided. In Donegal leadership was provided by the bishops. In the east it was Robert

Blair who provided leadership. All these leaders, of whatever religion, promoted their beliefs with great enthusiasm. This introduced an element of division among the settlers, which might otherwise not have come about. At Strabane it was a Roman Catholic layman that assumed the leadership.

Chapter 12

The Underdogs

So far attention has been given to the lords and ladies, but what of the simple tenant who relied solely on his ground to feed him. The typical "paddy" Irishman had to learn much from the migrants, and some written information has come down to us about them. Those who took up key administrative posts were responsible to the monarch. However, the undertenants have not been completely ignored. Their presence or absence on the various estates has given rise to the question of how good they were at managing the proportions or estates.

At the start of the plantation we have seen that the outflux from Scotland was considerable. These immigrants were mainly Scotsmen and they attracted the attention of the Venetian ambassador, who called attention to this fact in one of his dispatches. There were setbacks and even complete failure of some of the estates. The Scots continued to migrate into Ulster at a steady rate until 1619. After this date the flow of colonisers decreased. Who were these immigrants? Why did they leave Scotland for Ireland and from where in Scotland did they come?

The undertenants (the underdogs) may be divided into four categories: the gentry, merchants, artisans, and poor farmers. The settlement of Ulster was carried out with some degree of efficiency, but this was not to last. The Scots gentry were widespread in the north. Where the denizens specified the occupation of the applicant, the description of "gew" or "egg" was common. Sometimes the 1622 certificates gave certain freeholders and leaseholders similar titles. Abercorn remarked that many gentry resided on both Hamilton's and Montgomery's estates. The earl's observation is interesting, for in a letter he described the gentry concerned as of "gidfaschion". Later on these gentry sank to the level of the mere colonisers. Perhaps the second description was the more accurate as applied to the majority that came from Scotland.

The merchants were the most important of the Scots-Irish. The principal advantage of becoming a denizen was that property could legally pass to an heiress. The presence of merchants in the lists show that they quickly built up land in Ulster. It is almost certain that this property took the form of land. Hugh Hamilton, described as a merchant, leased sixty acres from Abercorn in free-farm in January 1615. It was Hugh Hamilton who probably imported delicious foodstuffs, for the rent was £6 sterling or one hogshead of Gascony wine, one pound of good butter, four pounds of loaf sugar and a box of marmalade containing at least two pounds of the preserve. The last item was said to be worth £1 sterling. The merchants thrived on the plantation as outlined through Robert Brown's records. In 1616, as an exponent of Irvine, he had gone to live in Ireland. Twelve other locations were entered into his records or book. Merchants and burgesses of this land frequently moved to Ulster, mostly settling in counties Londonderry, Antrim and Down. There was one instance of a burgess, a Robert Stevenson, living in Raphoe country.

Building works were much in demand as the plantation of Ulster went on its way. The supply of labourers was modest; the contribution of Londonderry and Coleraine was months before the first Scot arrived. Workers had to be raised from as far away as Munster and Connaught; alternatively they were brought over from England. Masons and carpenters followed in the footsteps of the colonists. Carew counted artificers amongst the British on Ochiltree's proportion in 1611, and six masons on Claud Hamilton's in Armagh. Two years later Bodley found a small number of masons from England and Scotland working on Claud Hamilton's estates in Armagh. Even builders that were not under the Scots distribution sometimes employed Scots. By 1611 the Scots were helping in the building of the new fort of Belfast.

Fortifications, like castles and bawns, were based on Scots designs with the characteristic corbelled turrets. Not all the efforts made in the plantation had come from Scotland. Some castles were built using Irish techniques, and Irish labour was widely used. Chichester remarked that if the Gaels were banished from Ulster, the building industry would suffer.

There is little written about the other types of artisan. Sir James Craig, as he defended the achievements of the colonisers, listed smelting, fishing, and tanning as being Ulster's most important industries. The Scots probably took part in these activities. The vast majority of artisans who went to Ulster must have been raised in one of the small towns founded by the undertakers. Local needs tended to be those of an agricultural society, as the towns grew up in the planters' atmosphere. The plan of one of these small towns can be gained from Lord Castlestewart's (Ochiltree) 1622 certificate. There was a total population of thirty leaseholders in Stewartstown — three gentlemen, three butchers, eight tradesmen, two weavers, two carpenters, three tailors, a ditcher, quarryman, shoemaker, malt-maker, smith, and schoolmaster. There were also three other householders whose occupations are not known. There were only a few masons, but otherwise this list was sufficient to run the plantation.

It was the ordinary tenants that made up the bulk of the plantation, but most of them had little money. Sir James Craig said that the poor British came to Ulster to settle with a view to making money. When the landlords increased the rents, many of the Scots could not afford their plots and had to venture to Scotland. The Scots undertenants acquitted themselves well, mostly in the years when the plantation prospered. Pynnar noted in 1619 that only the Scots were successful in ploughing the land. Without the grain harvest the entire population, British and Irish, would have had to starve. The 1622 commission at Strabane reported that the planters were full of industry. They *are very industrious, and doe daily beautify their Towne with new Buildings, strong and defensible.* The English settlement thrived to a great extent in County Londonderry. McClelland's colony was regarded as being the strongest and best able to defend itself. The Scots wrote about the situation at Armagh, and a plantation was proposed in 1622 for settling some land in County Monaghan.

Whatever their social origins, all of the undertenants possessed that common financial reason for going to Ulster, where they would also find status. If these goals were not realised they would return home. Montgomery considered that the wealthy classes that had settled in the province might double their worth. In this way the majority could attain to a superior position to the nobility of the homeland. One observer noted that tradesmen had become richer in four years in Ireland than during ten years in England. This was because of the cost of essentials. Before the plantation the official wages for master masons in Tyrone were set at 12d per day without food and drink. If the working week lasted six days this gave a weekly wage of 6s sterling, or over 1s more than in Scotland. The price of labour does not seem to have gone up as the planting went under way. However, there was an upsurge in demand, as we may assume that there was considerable prosperity in the north.

The greatest lure of all was the land. Sir Robert Gordon of Lochinvar in 1625, referring the poor settlers in Ulster (artisans and labourers, etc.) seems to have been confident about the task in Ulster. Sir Robert tried to get some of the Scots to emigrate to Canada. Sir Robert pointed to Ulster as the typical example of how the lower classes could reach out for prosperity. The same happened in English literature about colonisation in general. Ulster must have been already quite well off for this propaganda to be lavished.

Economics was the main motive for everyone, and this must have affected every immigrant. However, there were other factors governing the main plantation. The earliest colonisers out of sixteen planters were Robert Blair and Andrew Stewart. They said that the English and Scots settlers had had little to recommend themselves. Stewart regarded them as the keeper of the two nations. Blair agreed that the majority should rule, and, like all generalisations, this can be criticised. An attempt to organise traders had failed. These ideas were about forty years out of date. It has been thought that the first settlers in Ulster were fugitives from justice. King James had remarked that there were many batches of them putting down roots in Ulster soil.

More information about the Scots and English is shed only eight days after James wrote his letters on the subject. One letter is dated 1 August 1611 and it began by remarking that although the old ways of the Scots border had been suppressed, there was now the opportunity for a new beginning. New criminals pretended to be on the run and returned to England and their other origins.

Trade in many goods was combined with absenteeism, but otherwise order prevailed. The environment was relatively quiet, but it was out of these estates that the Protestant planters came. The explanation for this seems to be that there were high crime and unemployment levels on the land and in the little villages that were sprouting up in the escheated counties. Also, the export of stolen goods to Ulster began almost as soon as the plantation got under way. The criminal elements leaving for Ulster brought with them their ill-gotten gains. But the main purpose of the plantation was to stop crime and to contain the Roman Catholics. Early in 1612 the Council granted permission for the arrest of one John Hislop, who had, over a four-year period, started to ship large cargoes of stolen goods from Ireland.

Not all of the Scots had crossed to England after committing a crime. Irish justice may not have been able to contain them, but the local authorities were strong, and, despite the criminals, planters still took up their lots, small and large. There was the passage of slaves, goods and criminal persons. There were lots of planters that wanted to take up their positions. Many of the planters may have been Lowland Scots and border Scots. Most of the stolen goods had their origin in various parts of Scotland. The first police force appointed by the authorities was going under way. Both soldiers and cattle were in great demand amongst the colonisers. Grazing cattle was considered a good way of keeping the land and for establishing lasting law and order in the various plots. The tenants had targets of their own, and it is interesting to note that in 1612 King James received information from several sources that Sir Hugh Montgomery was harbouring criminal elements upon his lands. These were mostly Scots outlaws. Montgomery was exonerated, the accusations proving false, although some historians state that there was no smoke without fire.

The measures introduced into the Scots Council in 1611 had little or no effect upon the migration of Scots into Ulster, and criminal elements still troubled little harbours and set up shop upon the escheated counties. In 1613 Abercorn and Ochiltree were consulted about a ferry link between Ulster and Scotland. Trade would be supervised by the ports, but no immediate action was taken to implement the scheme. In the following year the majority in Wigtown in Galloway, Scotland, were ordered to arrest all those engaged in illicit trade, but these measures were of little value. At last a ferry link had been established between the little Ulster ports and the bigger moorings in the west of Scotland.

The 1616 scheme divided the Scots west coast into four sections. A system was set up to handle goods — with Whithorn, Portpatrick, Kirkcudbright and Ballantrae. The scheme served Carrick, and the people of Irvine and Largs, Glasgow and Galloway. Glasgow and Dumbarton were to be the official outlets on the Clyde. A competitive transport system had been set up. Planters were to show their handwriting and were to show testimonials to be available in the ports concerned. The sheriffs were to examine the position in the ports every quarter. The sheriffs of the counties involved were to examine the records of the ports. William McClelland of Overlaw, and John Cunningham of Raws were appointed to supervise the administration of the entire operation.

Similar means were being considered in Ulster. In a previous chapter it has been shown how in 1614 King James had given orders that Donaghadee should be investigated to assess its suitability as a port between Ulster and Scotland. It had great potentialities as a terminus for Anglo-Irish trade. The commission put in a favourable report. The Irish were subjected to effective colonisation in general. This seems to mean that the system of control was operative only on one side of the Irish Sea and North Channel. The 1616 measures seemed temporarily to have stopped unlawful planters from setting up shop in Ulster. One example of the new passport system has come down to us. It suggests that the proclamation was not simply an empty exhortation. Sir Hugh Montgomery, eight years later, could look back upon his plantation efforts with great pride.

In 1617 the border landlords requested permission to steal on their way to Ireland beyond the confines of the border counties. For five years there is no further reference to outlaws seeking refuge on Gaelic land or upon the plantation in general (excluding counties Antrim and Down).

By 1622 the control system had broken down. There was a great number of thefts taking place as people travelled between Scotland and England, and an inquiry showed that the Council could do little about the situation.

As a result of the influx of thieves, it was the Irish Council that acted first. On 21 September it issued a decree deploring the calibre of persons that had set out their plans for Ulster. Wanderers still poured into Ulster along with idle hands, but it was difficult to make out a case for imprisonment, for it could not be proven that these newcomers had criminal records. The Irish proclamation, it seems, never took effect, and two years later the Scottish government had to give in to a further consideration. But why did the Irish administration take action in 1622 when it took more in 1616? In 1624 Viscount Montgomery tried to obscure the explanation to the last part of the question, and it was decided that Donaghadee was the new terminus for traffic sailing between Ulster and Ireland. There was jealousy, probably emanating from Hamilton, and it prevented Montgomery from receiving a monopoly of trade. It still does not explain the publication of the 1622 proclamation. But there is a lot of speculation — first of all that it was issued just after the Commons had made their position clear in the province; secondly, it must be remembered that by 1622 the condition of the Ulster plantation was much to be desired. In the following year or so (up to 1618) fugitives from justice could find refuge in Ulster, and they were easily absorbed into the settlement. By 1622 rents were high and uncertainty of terms meant that land lost much of its appeal. In 1622 it had become as profitable to steal livestock from Ulster and ship it to Scotland. Those now entering Ulster found it difficult to settle down. Many planters, so Hamilton complained in the last year of the reign of King James, arrived in the north only to return to Scotland in possession of three or four horses. By 1622 stagnation had set in affecting the plantation as James's reign came to a close. The English government had to try to impose severe restrictions on Scots entering Ulster.

Even while the king sought means to stop outlaws from finding a house in Ulster, the government made restrictions as a punishment for crimes committed. But Ulster was not turned into a penal colony. The number of criminals in Ulster at this time amounted to only a fraction of the total immigrant population. The records show that some criminals were sent to Ulster on purpose.

The English had transported criminals to Ireland before the main plantation took place. In 1606 Graham, from the English side of the Scots/English border, had been forcibly sent to Connaught. It is not clear when the Scots had started to deport the criminals. No records of banishment are extant until 1620. The English submitted a petition to the government saying that there should be better government in the "middle shires". The Scots Council agreed in 1618, recognising the planters in Scotland as misfits. The flow of Scots at first was a trickle. Later the same year the Scots Council issued a decree that all wives and children of those who had been previously banished should join their husbands and fathers. Five men were deported to Ireland in 1620, and all five came from Dumfriesshire, the names of Johnston and Armstrong standing out, the fifth being an Ervine — all familiar border names. The five appear to be petty gentry, they settled in a particular place, and they had their critics.

The ministers understood the Ulster situation very well, for they were preaching to criminals who must have paid lip service for the sake of staying in possession of their lands rented from the Crown. The geographical origin of the estates is as important as the policies of the planters themselves. Criminals either left for Ulster of their own free will or were forced. Most of the Scots came from the border regions. The muster roll of c.1630 has given us a glimpse of what conditions may have been like. Some attempt is made to ascertain the position of the Scots in Ulster at the end of King James's reign. However, the figures cannot be checked and little is known about the authorship of the c.1630 muster. It has been used as a source for determining the origin of the Scots immigrants. The muster records many Scots names in various parts of Ulster. Tenants seemed to have moved around a lot. Those surviving in the 1622 certificates do not coincide with those of the muster for the same estates. There is a clear relationship between family names most clearly found in the certificates and those included in the muster. The conclusion can be drawn that there is no evidence to show that the origin of the Scots was much different between 1622 and c.1630. If one looks at the muster, it can be discerned that the immigrants with names associated with specific areas of Scotland very nearly settled near to one another. County Fermanagh is a typical example of this practice. Those names appearing most frequently in the county were Johnston, Armstrong, Elliot and Beatty — all border names. Other border names like Little and Irvine appear frequently in the muster. However, such names as Montgomery, Crawford, Cunningham and Hamilton are rare.

The newcomers granted lands to families with border connections, and this may explain why Ulster attracted so many Scots from this Scottish area. However, a close look at the rolls may lead us to a different conclusion. By 1630 slightly more tenants were living on lands belonging to one family than on the land owned by Lord Balfour. He had no connections with the border areas, but Balfour had a large number of tenants; Balfour attracted many Scots away from the lands owned by the Home family. It was Fermanagh's remoteness from Scotland and the immunity from Scots justice that had attracted the borderers. This may also explain why there were so many border names in County Tyrone, such as Eliott, Scot and Armstrong, even though the original grants of the Abercorn and Ochiltree families insure the planting of men with names such as Hamilton and Stewart.

There were the four escheated counties where the borderers did not dominate the settlements as they did in counties Fermanagh and Tyrone. The names in three counties were common in the western Lowlands of Scotland, and names did not outnumber each other. The exception was County Donegal where the Cunninghams and Campbells lived in great numbers. The presence of the former can be explained, for no less than five planters in this area possessed the name of Cunningham. Andrew Knox, Bishop of the Isles, cannot be held responsible for the large entry of Campbell immigrants, for they were not concentrated upon Church lands, but on the ordinary proportions. One may conclude that they were not Argyll Campbells, but came from Campbell country along the River Ayr.

The problem now arose of what to do with counties Antrim and Down. As in County Down the names of the chief landowners stood out amongst the tenants. In County Down no less than fifty-three Montgomerys and forty-four Hamiltons appeared in the muster for County Down. Next in the list for well-known names was Campbell. Like the Donegal Campbells, the tenants probably came from Ayrshire. They were mostly confined to the Hamilton estates. After the Campbells came such notable names as Johnston, Kennedy, Bell, Maxwell, Gibson, Dixon and McKee. Borderers (Johnson, Scot, and Maxwell) were represented, but it was the counties of Ayr, Renfrew, Wigtown and Lanark whose names made up most of the immigrants. The situation was the same in County Antrim where Stewart, Boyd and Hamilton were the three most common names.

Some Scots names were rare in Ulster — Gordon, Ogilvie, Grant, Innes, Fraser, Drummund and other names associated with the Firth of Forth appear infrequently. Names like Homes, Hepburn and Kerr, common names in the south-east, occur only occasionally. Now 14,000 Scots inhabited Ulster during the reign of King James I, known as the Jacobean plantation. They came largely from the eight counties which lay either along the English border with Scotland or up in the west coast of Argyllshire. These immigrants, as has been shown, represented a cross section of Lowlands Scots society. However, the poor, less well-off and less stable elements stood out.

Chapter 13

Traders, Migrations and Conclusions

At the end of the 16th century, trade had become a major factor between Ireland and the Scots ports. The other towns in Scotland benefited. If a fugitive was caught in Elizabeth's Ireland and arrested in Scotland, he was sent for execution, and the western burghers protested to King James that such favours to the English would jeopardise their position with the Irish. With the outbreak of the Tyrone rebellion, despite proclamations made in Scotland prohibiting traffic with the rebels, arms passed from Scotland into Ulster, which raised the value of goods between the two countries to fresh heights.

When the Earl of Tyrone, Hugh O'Neill, surrendered, the traffic war in contraband ceased; but, between 1603 and the beginnings of the plantation, in general trade took place between Ireland and Scotland and remained unaffected. In about 1598 Fynes Moryson described this trade as consisting of the exports from the Scots western ports of reed and pickled herring, some coal and whisky in return for imports from Ulster of yarn. To this list may be added Irish oats, barley, timber and fish. Sir Thomas Phillips said that in 1612, when Coleraine belonged to him before the plantation, the Scots came in great numbers; every summer there came between forty and sixty barks and boats into the River Bann, which brought merchandise and carried away timber and other commodities that were raised in County Coleraine. The volume of trade with Coleraine before the plantation was set up was considerable, and most of the trade was carried on with Scotland.

With the initiation of the plantation the volume of trade with Coleraine actually declined for two or three years. Phillips talked about the decline in the plantation after the Londoners had taken up their position. The Coleraine records bear this out. But they may have exaggerated the number of boats entering the River Bann when he arrived at Coleraine. He can hardly have doubled the figure, and a year later the Coleraine customs recorded only twenty-three ships (both English and Scots). Goods were taken in and out. It has been thought that the volume of trade between

131

Ulster and Scotland did not amount to much until the 1630s. This information is largely based upon the opinion of Fynes Moryson, who had been secretary to the lord deputy during the last years of Elizabeth's reign. He returned to Ireland after 1613 after a ten-year absence. He knew Ulster well from his service under Elizabeth, but he never saw Ulster during 1613. The purpose of his return trip was a visit to his brother who lived in the province of Munster in south-west Ireland. If he had toured Ulster during 1613, it is possible that he would not have seen too much trade between Ulster and Scotland. However, by the following year he would probably have found something upon which he could remark upon. In September 1614, forty vessels, twenty-six of them from Scotland, brought cargoes to Coleraine. This was a sure sign that the volume of trade approached the earlier level claimed by Phillips. Trade with Scotland was very much in the ascendant. The value of the total amount of annual imports nearly trebled during the three years for which figures are available. Those coming from Scotland increased by more than four times. Exports were also important and made even more spectacular gains. Those travelling to Scotland rose from practically nothing to £1,606 8s 9d.

At Derry trade benefited the plantation more than in any other place. Between the ten months from June 1606 to March 1607 custom receipts at Coleraine and Ballyshannon combined amounted to £35 3s 10d. By 1612-1613 these amounts had risen almost fourfold to £130 11s 8d for Derry alone. It was after 1613, however, that a striking increase occurred in terms of both imports and exports. The value of exports rose from £1,397 7s 6d in 1612-1613 to £9,935 8s 7d two years later. The other ports of Ulster were not as important as Coleraine and Londonderry. No records survive for the west of Derry. There was the position of Carrickfergus in County Antrim where trade was booming after the colonisers had established themselves. During the final years of King James's reign revenue amounted to £42 2s 10d. By 1614 the sum collected in any one year had risen to £234 13s 18d. There were bound to be errors in compilation, but the improvement was considerable. The value of goods entering and leaving Carrickfergus by 1614 had most likely exceeded £2,000. The levy on £1,789 10s 4d worth of imports into Coleraine between March and September 1615 amounted to only £92 10s 0d.

From the start the Scots entered into developing the plantation with great enthusiasm. Scots exports felt the effect of the immigrants. Colonisers who settled on Montgomery's land in County Down received two or three shipments per week after they had established themselves. At Coleraine, imports from Scotland exceeded exports until March 1615. Stolen livestock was sent to the province from Scotland once the plantation had got under way. Scotland remained not only a reservoir for the coloniser's supplies, but also a ready market for their produce. Prices for agricultural goods gave the colonisers a definite advantage. Prices in Ireland for food were not as high as those in England. In the Montgomery manuscripts Sir Hugh's first tenants sold their grain before leaving Scotland and bought more on their arrival in Ireland. This appears to show that the Scots prices were higher than those in Ireland.

The extent of trade in Ulster can be discerned by an examination of the Londonderry customs records. The Coleraine records are unreliable, but there was extensive trade between Londonderry and Scotland. In any one year, imports into Coleraine from Scotland never reached the halfway mark compared to trade at Londonderry. The value of exports from Scotland was striking. In 1614-1615, £1,662 1s 9d worth of goods left Coleraine for Scotland, and goods shipped from Scotland in the same year were valued at £4,368 5s 8d. Coleraine, however, did not provide a major outlet for goods to Scotland. The Scots of Mountjoy could as easily use Ulster's eastern ports to ship goods down the River Bann. Two of the most important Scots settlements in Ulster were at Portlough and the barony of Strabane. Extensive commercial relations grew up between Londonderry and Scotland during the three-year period, 1612-1615. Eventually the number of ships docking, bringing goods from Scotland, reached eighty-two in one year. Those exporting cargoes rose from eight to eighty-four. The Scots entered Londonderry with great frequency. Scots ships involved rose from fifty per cent of the total to about eighty per cent. By 1614-1615 the value of goods exported in Scots ships was more than twice that of goods carried by Irish and English ships combined. During 1614-1615 nearly half of the goods sailing in Scottish ships went to England, France or Spain. Exports bound for Scotland were greater than those for any other country. The number of ships bringing goods into Londonderry exceeded the number taking goods out. The value of imports amounted to but a small fraction of the exports. As early as 1612-1613 the value of the goods exported exceeded that of the goods imported.

More ships were involved in the Scots-Ulster trade for the years 1614-1615. This was to be a characteristic of the plantation as a whole. Very few ships from Scotland's eastern ports made the journey to Londonderry. They took their cargoes to England, France or Spain. To make the trade profitable the ships involved had to carry more than those trading with the west coast of Scotland. Most of the Scots ships were from five to twenty tons burthen, and these smaller ships tended to come from the Clyde ports. Large flotillas called in at the Clyde, whose western Scottish origins are known.

The Coleraine records reveal no precise assessment of shipping activity. Ships from Irvine docked at Coleraine the most frequently, but ships from Glasgow were also common. Ports on Ulster's eastern coast, on the other hand, traded a great deal with Largs and Ayr.

It is undoubtedly true that it was the Scots colonies that proved most profitable in Ulster. The Londonderry records make frequent reference to the Earl of Abercorn, Sir James Cunningham and other Scots undertakers, either bringing goods or selling them. Large amounts of goods were shipped between Scotland and Ulster, and included forty stone of iron worth £277, for Sir John Stewart. The *Hopwell* of Renfrew of six tons burthen arrived at Derry in March 1615 carrying one hogshead of vinegar, a half barrel of prunes, four dozen iron parts, one hogshead and two barrels of drinking glasses, twenty-five stone of iron, fourteen gallons of whisky, seven barrels of salt and one dozen glass bottles. There was also French wine, Spanish silks, tobacco, spices, brewing kettles, powder and lead, nuts, door and horse locks, bone, lace, bridles, stirrups, coal, and codfish.

The Scots continued to dress in a Scots manner but the import of native dress was an important part of the plantation trade. Nets and ropes were imported by one John Brown for the fishing industry. Imports at Londonderry were usually those commodities that were not native to Ulster. Other types of imports (for example, garden seeds, and shoes) entered the port according to the Coleraine records. The same holds good at Carrickfergus.

The type of produce used by the planters depended upon size. On 14 November 1614 the twenty-ton *The Gift of God* (of Strabane) sailed for the Clyde from Londonderry carrying great varieties of goods and produce. The River Foyle was navigable up to Strabane for quite large ships. The Earl of Abercorn owned those goods and sent a great number to Scotland. These consisted mainly of agricultural produce of one kind or another. During 1614-1615 the grain and beef accounted for nearly half of all exports to Scotland from Londonderry. The rest was made up of hordes of both domestic and wild animals, tallow, livestock, cheese, butter, malt, fish and a little timber. The same type of produce also went from Coleraine to Scotland. The four eastern ports of Strangford, Killough, Ardglass and Dundrum exported about £1,011 worth of goods to Scotland between January and September 1614; also £20 worth of grain (mainly oats and barley).

Records in Ulster ceased after 1615; we rely on information from the various sketchy dates that are available for some Scottish ports. The volume of Ulster-Scots trade continued at roughly the volume that prevailed in 1614-1615 until about 1619. After this there was a great decline. Thirty-nine ships left for the Clyde by November 1619. Previously forty-six vessels had left the Clyde with cargo for the port of Londonderry in 1614-1615. By 1619 there appears to be a decline in the volume of imports from Scotland entering Ulster. Ships also left for Coleraine and other Irish ports. By 1620-1621 a further decline had taken place in Scots-Irish trade. The December customs book for 1619 declared itself to be a record of the goods and merchandise entering Ulster from the River Clyde. All ships leaving the Clyde were checked at Dumbarton. The ships listed as sailing for Ireland were twenty-seven fewer than in 1618-1619. Scots exports to

Ulster that had left from the Clyde were now reduced to a trickle. There is not much evidence of trade going the other way. No figures have recorded Ulster's exports to Scotland after 1615. The argument would be difficult to refute.

In 1613 the volume of Ulster's exports to Scotland first became known. Harvests in Scotland alternated between fruitfulness and failure. There were therefore intermissions when grain could be supplied. Grain had been shipped to Ulster from foreign shores but without any risk of prices falling below a profitable level for home producers. There was a good harvest in 1617, followed by another, and more in 1619-1620. The good harvests did not alarm the landlords. On 26 November 1618 the Scottish Council imposed a new custom duty. For every boll of barley and wheat imported there was a levy of 8d on bolls on other types of grain. The duty was doubled in October 1619, remaining at the same level until October 1620 when the duty was again doubled. At this level it stood until April 1622, but there was a poor harvest in 1621. The Scottish Council took the attitude that the imposition of a high duty on traditional merchandise was justified by good harvests. The Council consisted almost entirely of landlords. New duties were introduced and these were fashioned to suit the all-landlord Council. The burghs took the opportunity of the bad harvests of the early 1620s to point out that they had to buy grain at the normal price, which was quite high. They now had to buy at three times the normal price. They declared that there should in the future be no additional rates imposed on grain imports. Now the landlords united to oppose the merchants. The Council was able to reach a compromise in April 1626, whereby it outlawed imports if the domestic prices fell below a certain level and exports if they rose too high.

However, within a year of the above compromise coming into effect the Council was obliged to ban the many Irish goods that were pouring into Scotland at the western and south-western ports. There was to be an increase in duty in 1618 that was to prevent grain entering Scotland from the Baltic. Irish grain competed favourably with Scots grain, as did that from the Continent. Most of the grain shipped from Ireland came from Ulster, but now the imposition of the Scots duties on grain hurt the colonisers. Pynnar has it that it was the Scots alone in Ulster who cultivated the land to any great extent, and it must have been Ulster that laboured under the introduction of the tariff.

An investigation by the commissioners in 1622 complained that although there had been good supplies of grain from the north of Ireland, which encouraged the plantation of Ulster, exports declined because of high duties. There were greedy landlords in Scotland whose rent was paid in corn. It finally concluded that if the previous rate was restored, the condition of the peasants (and colonisers) in Ulster would benefit. The report must have been made before April 1622, when the Scots Council reduced the rate of duty. Scots-Irish trade had been hurt most badly.

The Scots reduced the tariff in spring 1622, but this did not help the colonisers very much. The Irish farmers were no less threatening than the Scots ones. All sorts of goods were subject to duties when entering Scotland. The landlords in Scotland objected during November 1624 to the burgh's attempt to have new regulations imposed. As far as prices were concerned, this would benefit Ulster. Until 1619 the sale of grain had brought prosperity to the province, but this must have taken place during the last years of King James's reign. However exports had risen again in 1627.

The tariff was reduced in the spring of 1622 but this may not have helped the colonisers very much. During four years in Ulster the position in Scotland vis-à-vis landlords and tenants must have been very different. Between 1622 and 1623 there was a surplus of grain for export. Either in 1623 or 1624 the duty on foreign victuals entering Scotland was raised again, but the privy council has recorded no proclamation to this effect. Upon the imposition of high Scots duties on imported grain all trade with Ulster stopped. The customs records for the Clyde region show that was not the case. There was also the trade in stolen articles between Scotland and Ireland, and it must have been impossible to abolish or contain these activities. About twenty-six ports on the west and south-west regions of Scotland were recorded as being involved in trade with Ireland in 1624. There were few problems for the smugglers. The amount of grain exports from Ulster to Scotland hit all regions of the Protestant Ulster colony. It may well be that there was no substantial trade between counties Cavan and Fermanagh and Scotland.

The relationship between trade and migration is hard to describe. The story of the Ulster Plantation is a story of the Scots traffic in trade by sea and agricultural activities on the land, not to mention who owned the land now that the Gaels had been driven off their plots. Ulster provided a new home for the Scotsmen, for they were planting virgin territory. James was the leading light in the plantation's existence but he never set foot upon Irish soil. During the early years the planters enjoyed good harvests. However, there was a decline in the number of Scots entering Ireland. The plantation established a new order, and the Gaels were now directly ruled from Dublin Castle, the headquarters of British efforts in Ireland. Also, a middle class grew up in the little towns and settlements. It was not until 1633 that the flow of Scots into Ulster became great. The colonisation of Ulster in the reign of King James I has left a great impression upon the Protestants in the present-day six counties.

They came, they saw, but did they conquer?

Select Bibliography

A Short History of Bangor Abbey (North Down Heritage Centre)

Cyril Falls, *The Birth of Ulster* (Constable 1996)

Donald Gregory, *History of the Western Isles* (University of Carolina Press 1962)

I. F. Grant, *The Lordship of the Isles* (James Thin 1982)

J. P. Sloane, *The Plantation of Ulster* (MacMillan 1908)

James Steven Curl, *The Londonderry Plantation* (Phillimore 1986)

J. C. Beckett, *The Making of Modern Ireland (1603-1925)* (Faber and Faber 1966)

John McCavitt, *Sir Arthur Chichester* (Institute of Irish Studies 1998)

G. L. Bear, *Origins of the British Colonial System (1578-1660)*

Philip Robinson, *The Plantation of Ulster* (Ulster Historical Foundation 1984)

Rev H. J. Clarke, *Thirty Centuries in South-East Antrim* (The Quoto-Press 1938)

William Butler, *Confiscation in Irish History* (The Talbot Press)